Reconstructing the Classics

CHATHAM HOUSE STUDIES IN POLITICAL THINKING

SERIES EDITOR: George J. Graham Jr.
Vanderbilt University

RECONSTRUCTING THE CLASSICS

Political Theory from Plato to Marx

SECOND EDITION

Edward Bryan Portis
Texas A&M University

Chatham House Publishers, Inc.
Chatham, New Jersey

RECONSTRUCTING THE CLASSICS
Political Theory from Plato to Marx
SECOND EDITION

Chatham House Publishers, Inc.
Box One, Chatham, New Jersey 07928

Publisher: Edward Artinian
Production supervisor: Katharine Miller
Cover design: Antler Designworks
Composition: Bang, Motley, Olufsen
Printing and binding: R.R. Donnelley & Son Company

Library of Congress Cataloging-in-Publication Data
Portis, Edward Bryan
    Reconstructing the classics : political theory from Plato to
    Marx / Edward Bryan Portis
        p.   cm. — (Chatham House studies in political thinking)
    Includes bibliographical references and index.
    ISBN 1-56643-049-6
    1. Political science—History.   I. Title.   II. Series.
    BOGUS JA81.P873   1998
    BOGUS 320'.09—dc20   93-27199
                                                          CIP

Manufactured in the United States of America
10   9   8   7   6   5   4   3   2   1

To my parents

Contents

Preface to the First Edition

My intent in this book is to highlight the importance of the classics of political thought to political scientists and their students. A great many political scientists suspect that their colleagues specializing in the field of political theory are concerned with issues and problems largely irrelevant to their own. They are social scientists, whereas the theorists of the discipline, whether seen as philosophers, historians, or publicists, appear to be engaged in an essentially literary endeavor because of their preoccupation with interpretation of the classics. Indeed, political theory is often considered a competing approach to the understanding of political phenomena. Unfortunately, many political theorists happen to agree with this assessment, and to the extent they do, I suppose it is at least empirically correct.

It is not, however, theoretically correct. As discussed in the first chapter, everyone is a political theorist because it is impossible to discuss political phenomena without making important theoretical assumptions. These assumptions determine not only which questions are considered important but even which questions make sense. The indispensable benefit of the classics is to ensure that one is a conscious political theorist, which is likely to be a precondition for theoretical consistency.

Each chapter is intended to present a coherent political theory derived from the work of a classical political thinker. All chapters share a common organizational structure, a feature that should facilitate comparison, accentuating the distinctive implications of accepting one of these alternative ways of looking at political reality for understanding and evaluating political possibilities. All this is explained in the first chapter. Although each of the subsequent chapters can stand by itself, none should be considered a substitute for reading the work of a great political thinker. For those using the book in the classroom, I urge that it be assigned in conjunction with primary readings. The chapters are succinct, and I think students will find them useful and occasionally provocative interpretations.

A number of individuals did me the favor of critically reading various chapters. My colleague Adolf Gunderson read several chapters. My brother, L.L. Portis, made valuable suggestions concerning my treatment of Marx; Rachel Gibson scrutinized my rendering of Rousseau; and Tom Denyer made some helpful comments on the first chapter. Russell Gardner and Aaron Knight served not only as research assistants but also as advisers. Stephen Terrell also helped as a research assistant in the final preparation of the manuscript. My friends and former colleagues Art DiQuattro and Roberto Vichot read every chapter, as did my old friend and former teacher George Graham. Hal Bass, David Woodard, and Thomas Spragens evaluated an incomplete manuscript for Chatham House and made many useful suggestions. I have been fortunate to receive all this advice, but I failed to accept all of it, and there can be no doubt as to who is to blame for the book's deficiencies.

My wife occasionally gave me the benefit of a skeptical outsider's perspective. My children had nothing to do with the book, but like to be mentioned. My parents never read a page of the manuscript, but had everything to do with any of its virtues, and I dedicate the book to them.

Preface to the Second Edition

I would like to believe that the need for a second edition of this volume is indicative of substantial interest among fellow political theorists in my particular view of the nature and value of our endeavor. The
evidence, however, suggests only that the book has been found peda-
gogically useful. This is good enough for my publisher, and for that I am
thankful.

The most significant change in this new edition is the addition of a
chapter on the political theory of Thomas Aquinas. In light of the influence and power of his thought, I was derelict in not including such a
chapter in the first edition. Beyond this change, I have altered the most
obvious infelicities of expression and style and added references to a
handful of new works in the brief discussions of the literature at the end
of each chapter.

Once again I have been fortunate in the help I have received. Stephen Terrell served as an able assistant and insightful adviser. My colleagues Adolf Gundersen and Ruth Shively read a draft of the new chapter and made many useful suggestions, as did Nicole Canzoneri and
Anneliese Reinemeyer. George Klosko brought some valuable biblio-
graphic material to my attention. Finally, I would like to acknowledge
the help and professional competence of Katharine Miller, who supervised the production of both this and the previous edition.

Reconstructing the Classics

Great Books and
Political Science

Why Should Political Scientists
Read the Classics?

Western civilization is blessed with a long tradition of political thought, constituted by a number of works written at a high level of comprehensiveness and logical coherence. These works are comprehensive in the sense that political problems are addressed in general terms, as contemporary manifestations of the difficulties to which all political communities are liable. Consequently, the most challenging and plausible of these works have been pondered by educated political actors and commentators centuries after they were written. The great books of Western political thought did not achieve their status as classics because academicians considered them fine examples of scholarship and taught them to students. Instead, political actors and critics found in them useful or challenging arguments to justify or criticize existing political decisions or arrangements.

The classics of political thought are an indispensable component of a liberal arts education simply because their authors addressed themselves primarily to politically engaged intellectuals and intellectually sophisticated citizens. By understanding the reflections of each age's greatest sage, the serious student of political thought can gain a heightened appreciation of the possibilities and limits of political action. Because politics is a form of action and experience, rather than the recurrent, mechanical interplay of a set of mute forces, statesmanship depends much more on a sure sense of priorities and judicious habits than on technical proficiency. And even if statesmanship has become irrelevant to contemporary politics, understanding great works of political thought can at least be useful in clarifying the political values used to evaluate our condition.

If this reasoning is correct, all citizens would benefit from the study of the great books of political thought. Nevertheless, this book is dedicated to the proposition that political scientists in particular need to be well versed in the classics. Indeed, I am going to argue that it is almost essential for the success of their social science that they be so. As social scientists, political scientists have two distinguishing commitments that journalists, practical politicians, or governmental advisers—the kind of people the authors of the great books typically were trying to reach —will not *necessarily* share.

The first of these commitments is perhaps obvious and has been the source of much skepticism among political scientists concerning the relevance of the classics of political thought. This is the commitment to empirical verification. To verify knowledge empirically requires that beliefs about reality be formulated into hypotheses that can be tested by observation. Now it is perfectly possible to find interesting hypotheses in the classics that could be tested in a contemporary context. For instance, Machiavelli asserts that a "Prince" should take advice only after asking for it, but should ask for it often. One wonders to what extent presidents and other political executives must establish such a relationship with their advisers in order both to remain on top and to stay informed.

Be this as it may, the classics are not likely to be a very fruitful source of such hypotheses. Most of the authors of these great works lived in societies far different from ours. There is some reason to doubt that fruitful hypotheses relevant to our society will easily be found in discussions of Greek or Italian city-states, early modern monarchies, or even the early stages of the industrial revolution. If propositions from the classics are to be applicable to contemporary politics, they need to be very general and abstract, requiring a good deal of specification before they can be applied in empirical investigations of existing political practices. And in fact, these works are characteristically written at a relatively high level of abstraction.

In what sense, then, can the study of the classics of political thought be indispensable to the scientific study of politics? The answer is to be found in the second distinguishing commitment of social science, which is a concern for the systematic or interrelated processes that allow us to account for unforeseen and therefore unintended consequences. Scientists are not interested in simply accumulating a random assortment of confirmed hypotheses, and it is the very abstractness of the classics, their treatment of the political difficulties of their age as the result of the fundamental, inescapable nature of political association, that renders them relevant to the systematic or *theoretical* concerns of social science.

Before discussing why this is so, an example will help clarify the sense in which social scientists have theoretical interests not typically shared by other social observers. Every member of Congress and every journalist assigned to Capitol Hill knows that the committees of Congress exercise tremendous influence on the fate of proposed legislation falling within their respective policy jurisdictions. They will also understand that seniority, how long a congressman has served in Congress and on a committee, often determines committee assignments and influence within each committee. Legislators, journalists, and lobbyists have to know these things because they must confront on a daily basis the influence of committees and the power created by the rules of seniority. Yet, however intricate their knowledge of the rules of seniority, they have little immediate incentive to reflect on the aspects of the system of primary importance to political scientists. These include the weakening of the party leadership, unable to control committee chairpersons who owe their positions to seniority rather than support of congressional colleagues. This decentralization of congressional power in turn creates a power vacuum that does much to explain the increased legislative influence of the president in the twentieth century. Although these sorts of systematic consequences, usually unintended, can be of interest and in the long run of great importance to participants, the pressures of immediate threat and opportunity in a competitive environment force them to emphasize the short run.

None of the great thinkers discussed in this book had much to say about Congress; indeed, only two of them lived after the United States was founded. Nonetheless, the classics of political thought are almost indispensable in helping political scientists to see this kind of systematic consequence, to see "the big picture." To appreciate why this is so, it must be understood that everyone is a political theorist in the sense that we all must make fundamental theoretical assumptions whenever we think about political affairs. Even if one's interest is focused on a particular election, one obviously presumes that one knows what an election is, what a politician is, and what counts as a citizen. If one must presume meanings for these concepts, then one clearly must also have some idea of what a society is, what constitutes a government, and, most basic and important of all, what distinguishes human beings from other species. One cannot begin to think about political affairs without these fundamental, and therefore very abstract, notions.

These basic theoretical assumptions make it possible for us to integrate our knowledge, to see information about elections, legislatures, foreign policy, and the like, as details of a larger picture. Even though we all must make such assumptions, it is not really appropriate to say that we all have a political theory. For most individuals it would be more exact to say that the theory has them; most individuals cannot articulate the fundamental meanings they unconsciously presume. Although most people can come up with a definition of government if pressed to do so, they will in most cases readily admit that it is an inadequate definition that does not really capture what they mean when they use the term. Very few can state just why they consider themselves and others human, and typically they are embarrassed by any request to do so.

We do not have to articulate fundamental meanings consciously because we attained them largely by a process of acculturation. We do not have to say what we mean because we all mean much the same thing; we learn what our words mean when we learn to use them, when we learn to speak. Our theoretical assumptions, therefore, can remain largely unconscious as long as they are unchallenged or as long as they allow us to communicate effectively with our like-minded fellows. And as long as they remain largely unconscious, they remain the unquestioned, authoritarian rulers of our thought.

Although this state of affairs usually suffices for daily life, indeed may be essential for its harmonious spontaneity, it is absolutely unacceptable for social science. One reason is simply the commitment of any scientist to subject beliefs about reality to criticism, if not test. Another is the likelihood that unconscious assumptions will result in inconsistent classification or contradictory beliefs. Finally, if the synthetic commitment of social science is to be fulfilled, political science must be explicitly theoretical. If we are to comprehend the interrelations of political practices, we have to have a firm, sure grasp of what we believe are the fundamental characteristics they necessarily share.

What the classics of political thought offer to political science are conceptual options, alternatives to one another and to the unstated conventional wisdom of our cultural context. The latter is most important, for the only way to clarify and gain a critical perspective on our fundamental assumptions is to confront them with alternative viewpoints. We may, of course, reaffirm our faith in the intellectual foundations of our political culture. If so, our ability to analyze and relate aspects of our political experience in terms of these foundations will be greatly enhanced, and we will be doing it with our eyes open.

How Should Political Scientists Read the Classics?

What one is attempting to find in the classics of political thought is going to determine *how* one reads them. Put differently, what one is looking for determines one's "strategy of interpretation." Some sort of interpretive strategy is necessary because any written text must be interpreted, whether it be the Bible, a news magazine, or a cookbook, if for no other reason than the fact that words derive a good deal of their meaning from the context in which they are used. With contemporary news magazines or cookbooks, problems of interpretation are not severe because the authors are presumably taking great pains to use words in the manner accustomed by their audience. In works such as the classics of political thought, however, interpretation is always a problem because the authors are attempting to alter the way in which readers define words and at times even create new words because existing ones simply cannot be altered sufficiently to convey novel meanings. We cannot simply refer to a catalogue of what most people mean most of the time, as we do with a dictionary, to see what an innovative thinker means. We must attempt to find the meaning in the context of the author's thought, relating the words used to their function within the text.

An example might be appreciated at this point, and one is readily available in Jean-Jacques Rousseau's use of the words *government, democracy, state,* and *sovereign.* Rousseau believed that all real political societies rest on the commitment of subjects to subordinate personal interests to those of the community. Going further, he argued that rational legitimacy required that all legislative authority be exercised directly by citizens committed to the community rather than by representatives committed to the interests of citizens. To emphasize this rather radical point he called the people, when engaged in legislating, the "sovereign," and, when not (which is almost all the time), the "state." The "government" is defined as the organization that administers or enforces law, and in

Rousseau's scheme it cannot legitimately make law itself. "Democracy" is used to designate a particular kind of government, one in which all citizens have responsibility to administer the law, where there are no separate government workers such as police officers.

Rousseau pointed out the obvious, that "democracy" was an impractical form of "government" because we are not angels and will often fail to apply the law to ourselves without someone designated to remind us of it. Perhaps the resulting misinterpretation is now predictable. Some have mistakenly jumped to the conclusion that Rousseau declared himself an antidemocrat, neglecting to note that he was speaking of what we now call the executive function, rather than the legislative authority of the "state." Rousseau did not think it realistic in most communities for citizens to enforce their own laws, but he certainly affirmed that only they had the right to make them.

This example is an easy case of misinterpretation because Rousseau very explicitly defined his words in simple terms. He used other phrases (such as the "general will") that he could not define in simple, unambiguous terms because the meanings were novel and complex, and this is more typically the case. If a work did not involve novel and complex notions, it would not likely be considered a classic. Consequently, with such works we must look to the context, and how the context will be interpreted is in part determined by the purpose of our search.

As discussed in the previous section, what political scientists need from the classics of political thought are alternative conceptualizations of political reality, what I will call *conceptual paradigms*. The classics are often read for other reasons, with other goals in mind. Historians, for instance, are more likely to read these works either as reasoned expressions of the thought patterns typifying an age or as indicative of the intellectual disputes and cultural tensions influencing the evolution of Western civilization. As a consequence, the historian typically adopts a strategy of interpretation that looks to the author's intention, focusing upon the author's concern with his or her immediate social and political environment. In other words, historians look to what prompted the writer to write and what the writer hoped to accomplish by writing.

The historical strategy of interpretation is perfectly valid given its animating goal. But however suggestive and useful historical interpretation might be, it is not really appropriate for social science. The classics can be of crucial importance to political science to the extent that they can offer alternative conceptual paradigms. A viable conceptual paradigm is comprehensive in that it provides a vocabulary for characterizing political situations in general, giving clear conceptual distinctions that can be the basis of unambiguous classification and the more detailed specifications needed to apply the conceptual paradigm to more particular circumstances.

Consequently, in interpreting a work of political thought from a social scientific perspective, we should always remember that the task is one of logical construction, rather than historical explanation. The appropriate strategy is to assume that a coherent conceptual paradigm exists and that any variation in the use of key terms is due to unstated specifications made in applying the general concept to more particular contexts. In other words, we should attempt to integrate the author's use of terms into an ordered whole, unified by a limited set of basic, abstract concepts.

What is involved in this will become more apparent in the following pages, starting with the next section of this chapter. At this point I only want to emphasize that this task of logical construction cannot be an exercise in historical recovery because it almost inevitably involves reconstruction. Even a great thinker is susceptible to inconsistency, and justifiable veneration should not lead to blind emulation. More important, because more frequently relevant, is the fact that the great political thinkers were not addressing themselves to social scientists, and much of what is crucial to the latter may be present only by implication. *Because of the nature of the task, what authors should have written, given their basic conceptual assumptions, may be more important than what they actually wrote.*

There is another strategy of interpretation, which I will call the *philosophical,* even though it is not uniformly characteristic of philosophers. It sees a classic work of political thought as an effort to develop the social implications of a moral truth. Its aim is to derive a consistent set of principles that can be used to evaluate political events and guide political choice. The philosophical and social scientific approaches share an ahistorical perspective in that both look beyond the author's particular circumstances in finding the meaning of his or her work. For this reason, both interpretive strategies should sanction reconstruction if an author's words or clear intentions are incongruent with his or her primary tenets.

Despite this similarity in technique, there are critical differences in focus and orientation between philosophical and social scientific approaches to interpreting the classics. Scholars adopting the philosophical approach are addressing themselves, in effect, to judges. Because it is their task to provide clear principles that can delineate jurisdiction and justify judgments, they are concerned primarily with questions of political justice and political obligation. As a result, the philosophical approach is preoccupied with prescriptive principles, and questions of political stability, political possibility, and political ends are of secondary importance, if not completely irrelevant.

These latter questions are of chief concern to the politically engaged, which is why the social scientific approach to interpreting the classics is more appropriate for political science. Yet it is also more relevant to the education of citizens. The formulation and codification of principles are certainly valuable endeavors, but only after those who are to live by such a code have decided what kind of people they should be and how they need to organize themselves in order to be such people. In other words, political principles can be formulated only after political ends have been established. As the following chapters amply illustrate, the adoption of one conceptual paradigm over another has decisive implications for one's political priorities.

Some philosophers, however, believe that fundamental moral principles can be conclusively established through logical demonstration. From this view, our choice of a conceptual paradigm should be guided by these logically compelling principles, rather than the other way around. In general, there are two kinds of arguments for establishing such principles as undeniable verities of human existence: the *epistemological* and the *ontological*. An epistemological argument claims that we cannot deny a moral truth because it is a necessary precondition for our ability to think. An ontological argument claims that we cannot deny a moral truth because we would be denying the grounds of our own existence. Simply put, an epistemological argument says that we cannot deny a particular moral truth because we would not have the mental tools to claim or deny anything if it were not true, whereas an ontological argument says that we would not be here to deny it unless the moral truth in question were true.

Although I do not doubt that one must make epistemological and ontological assumptions, implicitly if not explicitly, and that these assumptions have at least indirect implications for personal priorities and social theory, there is little reason to believe that fundamental moral truths can be conclusively established through the explication of such assumptions. If they could, then political science would not need to concern itself with alternatives. It would need to concern itself only with the implementation of an established moral truth, and we could neglect most of the great books of political thought as a catalogue of errors relevant largely to historians.

What Should Political Scientists Look for in the Classics?

In view of the fact that the benefit provided for the political scientist by the classics of political thought consists of alternative conceptual paradigms, each should be interpreted in such a manner as to accentuate its uniqueness. But all comprehensive conceptualizations of political affairs must offer answers to the same set of fundamental questions, however distinctive and divergent these answers may be. The subsequent chapters of this book are organized around a set of four such questions, which I hope provides a basis to compare and contrast the alternative conceptualizations of politics that can be found within the works of the greatest political thinkers.

The first inescapable question is the most important because its answer provides the key to the others. This is the question of *human nature,* the answer to which consists of a defining characteristic distinguishing humanity from other species. This question would be neither difficult nor very important if it were acceptable to stipulate what is going to count as a human being simply by reference to a set of physiological features. But, quite apart from whether it is possible to find physiological or genetic identifying traits that each individual must possess to be considered human, very few, if any, of us would consider them an adequate definition.

For one human characteristic is the ability, perhaps even the propensity, to be inhuman. This somewhat paradoxical statement merely expresses the fact that humanity almost universally is considered a matter of degree, something to be maximized. We evaluate others, and indeed rest our own self-esteem, on estimates of how well the potential to be human is fulfilled. Such estimates are moral judgments, of course, and can be considered solely from a normative perspective. From a social scientific perspective, however, it is important that serious political thinkers do not limit themselves simply to prescription but argue that the failure to live as a human being has negative consequences for the individual.

They argue, in other words, that if one is able rationally to consider the consequences of living humanely or inhumanely, one would always choose to be human. Consequently, entailed in every sophisticated conception of human nature is a corresponding assertion about rational motivation. This is a theoretical rather than descriptive assertion, for people in fact do not always rationally consider the consequences and are motivated by what often are indefensible and even self-defeating wishes. The theoretical point is that there is, in such cases, a more personally fulfilling alternative that would have been chosen if a conscious, rational comparison had taken place. This allows the classification of alternative motives and the assessment of their relative worth.

The theory of rational motivation entailed in a conception of human nature has important implications for the second fundamental question addressed in all comprehensive conceptual paradigms. This is the question of *social solidarity,* or the factors leading individuals to accept socially imposed limits and sacrifices. There are undoubtedly many factors leading members of society to perform as necessary for the maintenance of social arrangements, perhaps simple inertia being among the more prominent. Other incentives will depend on the motives that typically animate people.

Because they can be defended, the reasons a fully conscious, rational individual would be compelled to be part of a social context will provide the most durable, if not the most frequent, of such motives. Given a particular conception of human nature, such an individual will value social intercourse to the extent that one has to be a social creature to realize one's human potential. Given that humanity is a matter of degree, however, not everyone can be assumed to have progressed sufficiently far in realizing the benefits of living a human life to be motivated by the desire to do so. Consequently, an adequate answer to the question of social solidarity must confront the issue of how it is possible for social life to accommodate a number of individual motives while giving primacy through encouragement to the most rational, the most appropriate and fulfilling for human beings.

Part of the answer to the question of social solidarity is likely to entail a role for government. This brings us to the third question, which is the *function and organization of public authority.* This question has two interrelated aspects. The first is perhaps obvious and consists of explaining what are the functions of authority, or why government is essential in a well-ordered, optimal society. The second aspect may be just as obvious, and this is the basis of legitimacy, or why a government has *authority,* rather than simply *power.*

On first consideration it may seem that any resolution of the first aspect, concerning governmental function, would simultaneously resolve the second, concerning legitimacy. This is not necessarily the case. For one may make a very good argument that a government is essential if important social goals are to be achieved, but fail to establish that individuals are either likely to acknowledge the point or even, if they do acknowledge it, to consider these social goals as important as their own personal goals. There is no great profit in constructing a "model" of a society in which rational individuals can maximize the realization of their human potential if it is a totally implausible construct. Such a theoretical model does not have to be probable to be valuable, but it does have to be conceivable. The model must be logically coherent even if its function is only to serve as an ideal to guide rational assessment of real-world options.

From a social scientific perspective, however, a theoretical paradigm must be more than simply a rational model. It must provide us with the general conceptual guidelines to make sense of existing as well as rationally ideal relationships and circumstances. To do so it must provide answers to the fourth question, that concerning *political change and stability.*

All political communities will encounter difficulties that strain resources and threaten established patterns of mutual accommodation. The sources of these difficulties are probably infinitely diverse and certainly unpredictable in the long run. The fundamental threats to a political community, however, are those undermining the ability to make effective collective decisions, especially those threats leading to a destruction of the very basis of legitimate authority. These are the causes of political instability about which one can have a theory because they take a finite number of forms, irrespective of the diversity of events provoking them.

They take a finite number of forms because there is likely to be only a limited number of motives that animate human action. Once one has isolated what one accepts as the defining characteristic of the species and thereby has committed oneself to a criterion of rational motivation, other motives will be sorted or lumped together in terms of their contribution to or compatibility with this standard. Just as there are personal consequences in failing to give higher priority to specifically human concerns, so too will there be consequences in attempting to legitimate authority by appeal to inappropriate aspirations. A regime failing to provide for human fulfillment will eventually have to cope with the behavioral consequences of frustration. Whether it is possible for such a regime to cope will significantly depend on its own unity and sense of purpose, and these attributes tend to be weakened by the same frustrations at the root of its problems.

The Structure of the Following Chapters

As indicated, these four questions are the focus of a separate section in each of the following reconstructions of the conceptual paradigms to be found in the most famous of the classics. These four main sections are followed by a brief concluding recapitulation of the implications of each conceptual paradigm for politics. Two additional sections, one at the beginning and one at the end, complete the common structure of the next ten chapters. The resulting seven sections are as follows:

1. The historical [thinker]
2. Human nature and rational motivation
3. The motivational basis of social solidarity
4. The function and organization of authority
5. [Thinker's] general theory of political change and stability
6. The politics of [thinker's ultimate political motivation]
7. A brief guide to the literature

The first section places each respective thinker in his time and place, emphasizing the circumstances under which he wrote his political works. Even though the task of interpretation from a social scientific perspective inevitably involves reconstruction, a knowledge of the author's intentions is an invaluable starting point, if not an infallible guide. The last section is an appendix to each chapter, including this one, presenting a very brief guide to some of the more notable commentary and alternative interpretations. The literature on each of these great political thinkers is vast, and little can be offered beyond a starting point for further investigation.

Since the final chapter is not concerned with a specific conceptual paradigm, it does not conform to this organizational pattern. It explores the normative implications of political theory in general and specifically the relationship between theoretical dispute and politics. I argue that the articulation of theoretical alternatives not only has the personal benefits discussed in this initial chapter but also entails a significant social benefit.

A Brief Guide to the Literature

There are numerous histories of Western political thought. The old standard is George Sabine, *A History of Political Theory* (1961), but at times Sabine is a more reliable historian than theorist. Leo Strauss and Joseph Cropsey's edited volume, *History of Political Philosophy* (1987), is more an encyclopedia than a history. The various essays are occasionally eccentric in their interpretations but are often thought provoking. Lee Cameron McDonald's *Western Political Theory* (1968) is generally informative and reliable. Nonetheless, in my opinion George Klosko's recent two-volume set, *History of Political Thought: An Introduction* (1993, 1995), is the best of the bunch. Two useful volumes that focus on modern political thought (i.e., since the Renaissance) are Dante Germino, *Modern Western Political Thought: Machiavelli to Marx* (1972), and John Hallowell, *Main Currents in Modern Political Thought* (1950).

For a social scientific critique of the study of political theory as the historical development of political thought, see David Easton, *The Political System: An Inquiry into the State of Political Science* (1953), chapter 10. Arnold Brecht, in *Political Theory: The Foundations of Twentieth-Century Political Thought* (1959), presents an extensive analysis of the disjunction between social scientific knowledge and the ability to make objective value judgments, and surveys past efforts to overcome it. Two sophisticated surveys of Western political thought also highlight the supposedly detrimental consequences of the rise of social science and its depreciation of traditional political thought. Leo Strauss, in *Natural Right and History* (1953), sees the development of social science as the result, beginning with Machiavelli, of the rejection of classical doctrines of natural order. The final product of this rejection, in Strauss's view, is a cultural crisis in which blind will displaces value, and nobody can really affirm anything about good and justice. Sheldon S. Wolin, in *Politics and Vision: Continuity and Innovation in Western Political Thought* (1960), does not condemn the idea of a social science, but attempts to demonstrate the negative implications for political judgment of thinking that all political knowledge must be social scientific.

I am attempting in this book to indicate the relevance of the classics not only to political evaluation but to political science as well. The most notable previous attempt to demonstrate the relevance of traditional political thought to contemporary political science is William T. Bluhm, *Theories of the Political System: Classics of Political Thought and Modern Political Analysis* (1978). In order to show continuity, Bluhm juxtaposes a classical author with one or more contemporary political analysts of note, although these contemporary figures are not necessarily committed to a social scientific view of political science.

Finally, for a sophisticated discussion of some of the complexities of textual interpretation, see John G. Gunnell, *Political Theory: Tradition and Interpretation* (1979). And for a contentious but interesting examination of the possible contingencies influencing the emergence of a work as a "classic" of political thought, see Conal Condren, *The Status and Appraisal of Classic Texts: An Essay on Political Theory, Its Inheritance, and the History of Ideas* (1985).

Plato and the
Politics of Beauty

The Historical Plato

It has been asserted that all Western philosophy can be seen as a foot-note to Plato, and in a certain sense the same can confidently be said for Western political thought. Plato's writings constitute the earliest surviving *comprehensive* discussion of the nature of political things. Although one can argue over what counts as comprehensive, and the experts can disagree over the historical facts, Plato may have been the first ever to present a coherent system of political thought. More important than temporal precedence, however, is that his writings display a degree of logical coherence and rhetorical persuasiveness that have rarely, if ever, been equaled. Yet very few of Plato's readers, in our time or his, have been able to accept his arguments concerning the rational organization of social and political life. Subsequent systems of political thought can be seen as "footnotes" to Plato, not because their authors followed or accepted Plato's starting point, but because they were forced to come to terms with his challenging alternative.

Plato was born into an aristocratic family of Athens in 428 B.C. and died eighty-one years later. He was one of a number of youths from well-situated families who became devotees of the philosopher Socrates. Indeed, most of what is known about Socrates comes from Plato, since Socrates himself did not write. No doubt already inclined from family background against the democratic forces dominant in Athens during this period, the execution of Socrates by a resurgent democratic regime when Plato was a young man made him a lifelong enemy of popular participation in public affairs. This event was clearly of crucial significance in Plato's development. Some of his earliest writings, in particular the *Apology* and the *Crito,* are concerned with the trial and execution. Moreover, Socrates appears in all Plato's writings except the last.

Socrates can appear in these writings because they are all in the form of a dialogue. Socrates engages in a discourse with others, often near contemporaries who were known by name and reputation to most Athenian citizens, of divergent opinions on fundamental matters. Through probing interrogation by Socrates, participants in the dialogue are led to reject former opinions as contradictory and perhaps to arrive at a logically defensible view of the matter in question. The *Republic* is the longest of these dialogues and the most important statement of the political implications of Plato's thought.

Given Plato's estrangement from the reigning political attitudes in Athens, his apparent abstention from active participation in Athenian public life is not perplexing. According to one of a number of letters attributed to him, Plato did attempt to take advantage of his close association with a powerful individual in order to implement his notion of a rational and just political order in another Greek city-state. This undertaking was a dismal failure. Whatever his influence, it was indirect, coming from his role as an educator. He founded one of the first institutions of higher learning, the Academy, which trained a number of influential statesmen and continued centuries after his death.

Human Nature and Rational Motivation

"Our pupils must not ... stop short of the final objective. They can do this as much in harmonics as they could in astronomy, by wasting their time on measuring ... notes against each other."

"Lord, yes, and pretty silly they look," he said. "They ... listen as carefully as if they were trying to hear a conversation next door. ... They all prefer to use their ears instead of their minds."

—*Republic*, bk. 7

Rationality provides a convenient characteristic by which humanity can be distinguished from other species, and most definitions of human nature explicitly or implicitly refer to our ability to reason. Mere calculation, however, cannot in itself supply an adequate conception of human nature. A number of other species seem to share the trait, certainly to a degree, and machines can do some kinds of calculation more efficiently than any animal. If one is to find a convincing criterion for humanity in reason, then one must refer to reasonable ends as well as to the logical operations by which ends are maximized.

For Plato, reason is its own end, its own reward. In reason is found both wisdom and beauty; in fact, reason is the basis of both wisdom and beauty. Obviously, Plato did not see reason as mere calculation. Instead, reason is the logical relationship of ideas, and ideas are the ultimate reality. Plato is an *idealist,* as opposed to an empiricist who believes that knowledge ultimately comes from sense impressions. For Plato, ideas are more real than the supposed things experienced through the senses to which ideas might refer. Not many people are idealists in this sense, and it is important to understand Plato's argument for his idealism if his political theory is to be understood.

One aspect of his argument against empiricism is epistemological. If ideas did not exist, we could not know or sense anything. Ideas do not come from sense impressions because sense impressions are useless without ideas. To use a simplistic example, only my idea of a chair allows me to see such divergent things as a baby's high chair, a rocker, a stool, or a large bag of beans as subsumed by this notion. They just do not look or feel or smell the same. So too with trees: Oak, pine, or palm trees do not look much like one another.

More relevant in the present context is the metaphysical basis of idealism. Plato maintains that anything that exists only temporarily must owe its existence to something more basic that does not change. Otherwise we would have to believe that things simply emerge from nothing and slip back into nothingness without rhyme or reason. Real or ultimate existence requires permanence. Temporal chairs and trees come and go, the only thing that might be universal and persistent about them is the idea of a chair or tree. The idea, therefore, is more real than the temporary instances accessible to the senses. Knowledge of reality is knowledge of ideas, their interrelations and logical implications.

For purposes of illustration, ask yourself who has the superior knowledge of automobiles: the garage mechanic who learned his or her trade through apprenticeship, or the mechanical engineer trained in a university and employed by a manufacturer to design autos. From Plato's perspective we must say the engineer, even if the individual in question were incapable of servicing his or her own car. In order to diagnose and repair the autos on the road, the mechanic must know how cars generally work, but more important is an intricate familiarity with a large number of existing automobiles and a mastery of the proper procedures to fix or replace parts in each type. However useful such knowledge of specific instances is to those who oversee the creation of autos, the truly decisive expertise comes from the ability to see an auto in the abstract, as a system of interconnected systems: the power source, the drive train, the braking system, the fuel system, the electrical system, and so forth. To the engineer a car is not a concrete thing, greasy inside and shiny out, but a set of abstract specifications. If it were not for the idea of an auto, neither autos nor mechanics would exist.

So too with everything else that exists. We know only through ideas. The advance of science, a modern Platonist would argue, takes the form of comprehending the underlying necessities behind the apparent contingencies of experience. Molecular theory, for instance, is highly abstract, best expressed in the idiom of mathematical formulas. All advanced science depends on mathematics, just as mathematics depends on formal logic. Formal logic, in turn, depends on more basic and abstract ideas, and if we are capable and sufficiently disciplined to pursue this ladder of abstraction, we would eventually reach the ultimate source of both knowledge and reality, the idea of the idea.

Plato held that only very rare persons can attain such absolute knowledge, and these he called philosophers or the lovers of wisdom. Being the most rational of humans, they are the most human. What is important from a social scientific perspective, however, is that Plato claims they are the happiest of humans. As discussed near the end of the first chapter, the great political thinkers derive a view of rational motivation from their characterizations of human nature. Plato asserted that those of us who live up to our rational potential would live happier, more meaningful lives than those who do not for two reasons. The first is that knowledge of the real is meaningful in itself. It is the source of all real beauty, and the philosopher's ability to comprehend the ultimate nature of reality allows him or her to experience the highest form of pleasure through such comprehension.

Plato assumes that harmony is the source of lasting aesthetic value and, as we should expect, harmony is an intellectual, rather than sensual, characteristic. For purposes of illustration, let us again pose a question: Which is the superior form of Western music, classical or popular? Plato of course was familiar with neither, but there can be little doubt that he would consider Mozart, Beethoven, or Shostakovich far superior to Frank Sinatra, Hank Williams, the Beatles, or your current favorite. Classical music has a timeless quality because it develops themes that can be appreciated irrespective of how they are interpreted by different musicians. Indeed, because he was deaf when he composed it, Beethoven never heard his famous Ninth Symphony. Moreover, those who have a sophisticated grasp of musical *theory* can enjoy the beauty of this and other great works of the classical tradition by reading rather than listening to them. Can the same be said for *most* popular music? The sound, the style, and the lyrics would seem to be crucially important to most currently popular songs. They express the emotions or sentiments of a particular population at a particular time. Even "golden oldies" owe their longevity at least as much to nostalgia as to permanent aesthetic appeal.

Genuine beauty, like the reality it expresses, never dies. This is true in music, architecture, science, or mathematics. Beauty, like truth, is found in order, and for an idealist all order is ultimately intellectual. In a manner only hinted at in our appreciation of the "classical" unity of the Parthenon (long since stripped of the silly decorative statuary Plato's foolish contemporaries attached to it) or the sense of pleasure derived from an elaborate yet clever mathematical proof, Plato's philosopher loves wisdom because the abstract intellectual unity of reality provides the greatest possible aesthetic experience.

A second, more negative, reason the philosopher will be the happiest of individuals concerns the difficulty most of us have in setting priorities for ourselves. This is because there are multiple sources of pleasure, even for a philosopher. In addition to a diversity of appetites associated with our senses, we also experience pleasure when we gratify basic psychological urges such as aggression or affection. All of these alternative sources of pleasure are instrumental in solving the practical problems encountered in coping with our social and physical environments. Each can become harmful, however, if pursued too far beyond these practical requirements. The satisfaction we feel at the relief of hunger, for instance, is functional to the survival of the organism. If carried to the point of gluttony, it becomes dysfunctional and even painful.

Unfortunately, the dysfunctionality of the unlimited pursuit of many other instrumental pleasures does not reveal itself so readily, and ignorant individuals often condemn themselves to such futilities as a meaningless quest for fame or a "joyless quest for joy."

The only pleasure that will not eventually become pain is the beauty achieved through understanding. This is the only pleasure that is meaningful in itself. Of course, the philosopher, like everyone else, must cope with his or her environment, and will gratify the host of mundane urges entailed in daily life and experience their attendant pleasures. The difference is that the philosopher will confine such pleasures to their appropriate, instrumental sphere. The philosopher's understanding and the appreciation of the pleasure of true beauty that comes with it allows such an individual to establish clear, logically defensible priorities.

The ignorant individual, in contrast, cannot establish clear priorities without help. Without this help, such an individual will be dominated by momentary urges. Indeed, since these urges are pursued without reason, they have the tendency to become blind, self-defeating addictions, especially in spirited, independent personalities. Help can come from two sources. The first is through faith in a higher order, usually expressed through religion and conventional social morality. Unfortunately, spirited, independent personalities tend to be skeptical of religious authority and social conventions. They and those whom they might mislead can be helped only through education. Naturally, only those with real knowledge of rational priorities can provide this education. Consequently, the second and more certain source of help is philosophy.

The Motivational Basis of Social Solidarity

Those who have no experience of wisdom and goodness ... never ... achieve any real fulfillment or sure and unadulterated pleasure. They bend over their tables like sheep with heads bent over their pasture and eyes on the ground, they stuff themselves and copulate, and in their greed for more they kick and butt each other ... because they are not satisfied.
—*Republic,* bk. 9

There are, in general, two reasons people voluntarily accept social limitations and obligations. The most basic, if not necessarily the most important, corresponds to the diverse needs whose gratification leads to the various forms of sensual and emotional pleasure. Such elementary needs as nourishment, shelter, clothing, security, entertainment, and affection are much more effectively gratified through social organization than isolated individual effort.

This rather obvious advantage binds individuals to society in two ways. The first is simply the dependence that individuals will almost inevitably develop toward any consistent source of benefits. It does not require a great deal of calculation to recognize the heavy costs of social isolation. The second is equally straightforward. The advantages of social organization over individual effort is achieved by the specialization, or division, of labor, and individual specialization is for all practical purposes equivalent to social interdependence. Individuals could not leave society even if they were foolish enough to want to do so.

Plato, however, argued that these essentially economic factors were inadequate in themselves to generate a sufficient degree of social commitment to support long-term stability. If individuals were motivated solely by gain, they as a matter of course would violate social conventions whenever such behavior was personally advantageous. Neither the farsighted anxiety of what would happen if everybody ignored the rules nor the immediate fear of detection would suffice to maintain social institutions if their sole justification were the satisfaction of mundane needs.

Consequently, the other, noneconomic reason provides the most essential basis for social solidarity. And this is the help that the vast majority of individuals require in order to establish a consistent set of priorities. If individuals are to lead even minimally satisfactory lives, they need to impose discipline on their multifarious, demanding, and often contradictory urges. In the absence of true knowledge of genuine beauty and worth, the only source of such discipline is social convention and expectation. Even in the absence of the ability to defend conventional morality or conventions, most individuals will stubbornly cling to their faith that the moral basis of their society possesses some sort of transcendent validity. In the face of ignorance, blind faith is necessary to maintain a degree of self-control.

The Function and Organization of Authority

"If the philosopher is compelled to try to introduce the standards which he has seen ..., and weave them ... into the habits of men both in their private and public lives, will he lack the skill to produce self-discipline and justice ... ?"

"Certainly not."

"And if the public discover that we are telling the truth about philosophers will they still ... disbelieve us when we say no state can find happiness unless the artists drawing it use a divine pattern?"

" ... They will stop [disbelieving]."

—*Republic*, bk. 6

A number of practical tasks clearly require institutions for collective decision making. Defense is the most prominent of this sort of task, which also includes maintenance of public facilities such as, to name some obvious examples for contemporary societies, harbors, roads, currency, and educational system. More fundamental than these admittedly important practical tasks, however, is the need both to express and to protect the conventional morality on which subjects rely to establish a sense of priorities and self-control.

For despite the dogged clinging to conventional morality characteristic of most people, governmental authority is needed to ensure the continued existence of a common morality. There are a number of reasons for this necessity, but in general they all stem from the fact that morality is ultimately accepted on the basis of faith, rather than rational demonstration. For this reason alone, the extent to which individuals will consistently conform to moral rules will vary considerably. If each could see that a moral rule was as logically evident as $2 + 2 = 4$, then transgressions would be as infrequent as the refusal to accept the results of arithmetic. In the absence of clear demonstrability, almost all will be at least occasionally tempted to take advantage of opportunities to gratify personal desires at the expense of "higher" values.

Since the belief in these higher values rests on mere faith, the proliferation of deviant behavior can only call their plausibility into question, especially for the relatively irresolute. A common faith thrives on reinforcement, but decays with neglect or conspicuous indifference. Consequently, governmental authority has as its most fundamental function the reinforcement of a common morality and the creation of disincentives for disregarding its code of behavior. The former it does through ritual, rhetoric, propaganda, and education; the latter, through law and punishment.

Existing governments have only limited, temporary success in accomplishing this fundamental task. From Plato's perspective, social instability and widespread personal anxiety are inevitable as long as the rulers are as ignorant of true priorities as their subjects. Various institutional mechanisms may be devised to ensure that those who rule best understand and are devoted to the common faith. Nonetheless, discord and corruption are inevitable just because it is a faith, rather than logically based knowledge, that they are supposed to defend. Quite apart from the difficulties of dealing with both skeptical and irresolute segments of society, the rulers will necessarily have differences of opinion over the exact meaning and implications of their common faith. In other words, without an objective logic to resolve disputes in a rational manner, internal discord will lead to political struggle and will undermine the effectiveness among those entrusted to protect the common faith.

Chronic disunity among the leaders of the faithful is not the only, or even the most decisive, factor ensuring social and personal misery. Much worse is the certainty that many of these leaders will eventually become corrupt, irrespective of institutional arrangements intended to prevent this from occurring. A number of reasons could be given for the oft-repeated adage that power corrupts, but they all come down to the rather simple observation that power brings a number of advantages that tempt leaders to place the preservation of their own status above their responsibility to the public good. Not everyone, naturally, will succumb to this temptation, and given the proper institutional safeguards it may be possible to protect the public good even with a limited degree of political corruption. But this presumes that corruption can be confined to some limited degree, and this is exactly what Plato would deny. For we can be confident only of those individuals with clear and *defensible* priorities. For them, temptation will be no more than a form of foolishness. For those whose higher moral priorities are a matter of faith, only their fear of losing direction, of losing control of themselves, will give them the courage to resist. Unfortunately, power tends to encourage self-confidence, rather than humility. Leaders tend to look at themselves as exceptional, rather than susceptible. Their dispositions, their opportunities, and especially their ignorance work together to circumvent even the best institutional constraints.

Since we can be confident only of those with clear and defensible priorities, obviously it is these whom we should want to rule. The only individuals able rationally to defend ultimate priorities are Plato's philosophers. Moreover, we could be certain that a true philosopher would be incorruptible because he or she is capable of enjoying the greatest of all pleasures, the appreciation of absolute beauty. Power can offer nothing competitive and therefore nothing to tempt. Indeed, one of the more troublesome problems with Plato's political thought is the question of incentives for his philosopher rulers. If they are able through their own contemplation to enjoy the highest, most meaningful pleasure, why would they accept the burdens and distractions of power? His most plausible answer to this question is that they would do so because of their love of wisdom. For if they refused to organize society according to true priorities, then attempts will be made to organize it according to false priorities. That these attempts eventually will be futile is less important than the fact they are based on false premises.

Rule by philosophers would require the transformation of the community into an institution of education. Not only would this help to reconcile those committed to a life of knowledge with the responsibilities of power, it also would be required in order to ensure that true philosophers actually rule. Although Plato suspected that intelligence was at least partially hereditary, he recognized that all social strata produced potential philosophers, and that all produced fools. The vast majority lies somewhere in between, but many more are situated at the foolish end of the spectrum than the philosophical. In fact, only a minuscule portion of any population is likely to have the natural intelligence and discipline necessary to become a philosopher in Plato's sense. Consequently, one of the primary functions of the philosopher rulers would be to find those capable of joining and eventually replacing themselves.

We need not consider the detailed procedures that Plato recommended to train and test society's youth, shunting those unable to excel at each successive stage toward practical vocations suitable to their talents. The notable point is that a completely successful implementation of such a scheme would result in the education of every individual to the limit of his or her ability. Although Plato is a thorough elitist, his meritocracy is based on complete equality of opportunity. More important, the system would ensure that every individual would develop his or her potential for living a human life, enjoying to the extent possible the higher forms of pleasure associated with reason and, to the extent it is needed, the security of a reassuring moral environment.

For the educational machine to work, the voluntary cooperation of all, no matter how lowly the practical occupation assigned to them, is essential. On the surface it would seem reasonable to raise the question whether the subjects, forever denied the right to participate in the making of collective decisions, would tolerate their exclusion. Plato brings forth a number of considerations explaining why this would not be an unmanageable problem in a rationally ordered system. The first consideration is that the rulers would not be resented because they would not be seen as threatening. The rulers would not be interested in riches or the things that riches can purchase just because they know a greater source of happiness. Nor would they flaunt their political status as something to be envied. They rule, after all, as a matter of onerous duty, rather than great privilege.

In fact, in a well-ordered system the philosopher rulers would not own private property or even have families. They would live as monks in a monastery, devoting themselves to philosophy when they could and to public affairs when they must. Once again, we need not discuss the procedures Plato envisioned by which they would mate and raise their offspring or other details of their daily life. The relevant point is that such individuals would only be distracted and annoyed by many of the things in which most of us take great pleasure merely because these are among the limited pleasures open to us. Simply put, the subjects would not choose to live as the philosopher rulers, and if that were seen as the price of power, they would not want to pay it.

Yet this raises another apparent problem with the likelihood of popular support in such a system. Would the arrangement really make sense to the subjects? For if we saw the rulers' lifestyle as a "cost," would we be convinced that they really were able to see a great beauty that our natures deny to us? Would we be willing to acknowledge that our pleasures are limited, rather than great? Plato believes so. The first reason should be obvious at this point. We want to believe because we need to believe in the rationality of an objective set of moral priorities, irrespective of whether we can defend it ourselves. There is another reason, just as decisive and yet more positive than our dependence on and need to maintain faith. This is simply that we are rational creatures even if we are unable to be philosophers. We, too, can appreciate the permanent beauty and power of ideas. Most of us recognize the superiority of "serious" music, literature, and occupations. Even though we may occupy ourselves primarily with less demanding pursuits and entertainment, we appreciate and even prize our exposure and limited abilities in the higher forms of knowledge. We respect those who through ability and self-discipline have mastered serious things. Most important, we appreciate their efforts to give us some idea of the (to us) "complexities" of nature so that we too might experience some of its fascination. We need not presume to be the equals of our mentors in order to value their knowledge and place ourselves under their guidance.

Plato's General Theory of Political Change and Stability

You must find for your future rulers some way of life they like better than government.... If you get ... men whose life is ... destitute of personal satisfactions, but who hope to snatch

25

some compensation for their own inadequacy from a political career, there can never be good government. They start fighting for power.

—*Republic*, bk. 7

Change in political institutions can result from diverse causes, and an all-inclusive theory of political change is probably less likely than a similar theory of weather. As noted near the end of the introductory chapter, however, fundamental political change affects the ability to make collective decisions, rather than the nature of the particular problems facing a public. It involves the ability to respond, rather than the success of the response. It is essentially a question of the ability of governmental leaders to gain acceptance as legitimate authorities who should be obeyed voluntarily. Any conceptual paradigm, having provided an outline of rational obligation and authority, at least implies the weaknesses of irrational political systems that will eventually lead to political instability and futility.

More problematic is whether a conceptual paradigm also implies guidelines for political development, the implementation of a rationally legitimate political order. Plato gave every indication of being rather pessimistic and had much more to say about instability than development. In fact, given the ubiquity of popular ignorance and the prevalence of ambitious, corrupt leaders, the only realistic hope of instituting rule by philosophers is by luck. One certainly could not expect the philosophers themselves to work for it. Some sort of dictator, one who inherited the position, rather than fought his or her way to the top, would have to have developed philosophic tendencies, perhaps under the influence of philosophical tutors or advisers.

Although such a fortuitous set of circumstances would be a rare event, the frequency of dictatorship might be sufficient to keep the hope alive. For Plato argues that existing political systems, based on a common cultural faith, rather than real knowledge, are inherently unstable and inevitably decline into tyrannies based on raw power. Political communities based on faith can be rank ordered into four types: *timocracy*, based on the love of honor through courage in the service of the state; *oligarchy*, based on love of wealth; *democracy*, based on love of liberty; and finally *tyranny*, based on nothing more than love of self and fear. Each stage degenerates into the next lower stage because, over the long run, no one can defend the values on which it is based.

This is a cultural theory of political change, and it has two interrelated aspects. The first is the corruption that inevitably undermines faith. Commitment to any value requires the subordination of other desires, and as long as the commitment is a matter of faith, these subordinated wants constitute an ever-present source of temptation. The timocratic citizen will secretly wish for the security that possessions can buy, the oligarchic citizen will wish to consume rather than produce, and the democratic citizen will wish to dominate in order to pursue intense pleasure, rather than be confined to the limited, even petty pleasures compatible with respect for the liberty of all.

Even if it were possible to keep corruption limited and the leadership in the hands of those truly devoted to the professed values, dissension among the latter would be a recurrent source of instability. Perhaps in itself, this source of instability would not be fatal, in that regimes of these three types could at least persist. Unfortunately, the second aspect of Plato's theory of political change precludes their survival in even a less than optimal condition. For it is one thing for the faithful to manage dissension among themselves, but quite another for them to justify this faith to their skeptical children. Given the inevitability of temptation and corruption, it is also inevitable that the brighter, more spirited youths who demand consistency between belief and life will look on the corrupt wishes as more real than the received faith. The latter, in fact, will look increasingly as an irrational facade incompatible with the apparently more natural wishes that are unsuccessfully repressed. Perhaps as a result of having to live in someone else's world, youth always has a keen sensitivity to hypocrisy.

The combination of internal dissension among an increasingly aged faithful and a rising generation that makes a virtue of what was formerly considered corrupt will inevitably prove fatal to regimes based on these sorts of values. The process is likely to be marked by fits and starts, and there will be restorations as well as coups and rebellions. Fundamental change, just because it is the result of cultural transformation, will usually require a number of generations to be complete. In the complex mass societies of the present, political culture is probably always a mixture of types, and all that changes is its central tendencies. From Plato's perspective, for instance, we probably could say that the United States had an oligarchical political culture with democratic tendencies through much of the nineteenth century, but in the course of the twentieth century it became a democratic culture with oligarchical tendencies.

If this is a valid characterization, and if Plato's analysis of the inevitability of decline is correct, we should expect in coming decades to see an increase in political discord and the rise of popular political leaders ready to disregard constitutional limitations. For Plato argued that all regimes based on mere faith degenerate into tyranny, and democracy represents the last step. Ambitious leaders gain popularity through use of public resources, which requires heavy taxation of the wealthy. As the wealthy conspire to protect their advantages, the masses come to look on their ambitious leaders as protectors. Clinging to their positions at all costs, the leaders are forced to manufacture both foreign and domestic enemies of the people in order to protect their status as protectors. In time, the leaders resort increasingly to terror and must eliminate all who might provide an alternative to themselves. This includes not only other ambitious leaders but also anyone of obvious ability and integrity who might be seen by the disaffected as an alternative. Tyranny is the opposite of rule by philosophers; it is rule by those who fear the best, who must persecute those capable of pointing the way to truth and genuine beauty.

Political development, as opposed to political decline, can only come from the chaos of tyranny. Eventually a tyrant will consolidate his or her power, and perhaps through family or a coterie of trusted underlings attempting to hang on to privileges after the dictator's natural or unnatural demise, a new common faith is fostered. Plato had nothing to say about this process, but something of the sort would seem to be the only way the higher forms of regime could be established before beginning the long trek toward tyranny. What kind of faith is adopted undoubtedly would depend on circumstances and individuals. Yet from this uncertainty emerges the possibility, however slight, that those who have the advantage of objectively valid priorities can guide us toward social harmony and personal appreciation of the beauty of reality.

The Politics of Beauty

Moral principles serve the crucial psychological functions of controlling our appetites and harnessing our energies. Most individuals derive their moral priorities from social convention, and the most important task of political authority is to protect the common faith that sustains the community. Yet only those whose priorities are derived from knowledge, rather than convention, can be reliable interpreters of the common faith. Furthermore, only they will be trustworthy guardians of its integrity.

Tragically, the desire to rule is inversely related to the ability to do so. Those who think that being guardians of the community is meaningful in itself will look on a common faith as a means for individual advantage, rather than a higher end and a trust. The politically ambitious make the worst rulers, and yet they are the most likely to rule. Although Plato places no faith in the dependent masses, those of us unable to comprehend the fundamental nature of existence would do well to entreat the wisest among us to rule. Our only condition should be that they lead us to appreciate, insofar as our individual natures allow, the beauty of reason. If they refuse to do so, we can be sure that they are not true lovers of truth.

A Brief Guide to the Literature

Because of the meagerness of historical sources, we will never have a useful biography of Plato. For a brief, straightforward discussion of what historical evidence exists, as well as a remarkably concise and readable introduction to Plato's thought, see A.E. Taylor's *The Mind of Plato* (1922). A useful overview focused specifically on Plato's political thought is provided by George Klosko, *The Development of Plato's Political Theory* (1986). More controversial, and certainly more speculative, is Ellen Meiksins Wood and Neal Wood's attempt to see Plato's thought as an ideological justification of class privilege, *Class Ideology and Ancient Political Theory* (1978).

No one doubts that Plato was critical of Athenian democracy. Yet, however elitist, the political doctrine advanced in the *Republic* is on the surface quite radical. Philosophers should rule, and they should be guided by reason, rather than social convention and tradition. Plato clearly realized, for instance, that his readers would be shocked by his assertion that women would be among the rulers in a rational state. Such a notion violated the Greek view of the family, as illustrated in Susan Moller Okin, *Women in Western Political Thought* (1979).

A number of commentators of conservative inclinations have argued that Plato did not really intend for his more radical statements to be taken literally. One must probe beyond the surface if the *Republic* is to be understood, especially since we are dealing with a dramatic dialogue, not an expository treatise. Foremost among these commentators is Leo Strauss, who in effect argued that Plato's purpose was not to prescribe a certain set of political arrangements but to establish the priority of philosophy over politics as a way of life, and the danger that the latter always presents to the former. Strauss's ideas on Plato are perhaps best presented in *The City and Man* (1964). A trenchant critique of these views is presented by M.F. Burnyeat, "Sphinx without a Secret," *New York Review of Books* (1985).

Given his disdain for opinions derived from observation and experience, a degree of animosity toward Plato by the champions of social science is to be expected. Perhaps the most negative analysis of Plato's influence is presented by the famous philosopher of science Karl Popper. In *The Open Society and Its Enemies* (1957), Popper argued that Plato's belief in the existence of ideal forms led him to view all social change as degeneration, and that these beliefs planted the seeds of totalitarianism in Western thought. A more balanced appraisal from a social scientific perspective can be found in Alvin W. Gouldner, *Enter Plato: Classical Greece and the Origins of Social Theory* (1965).

3

Aristotle and the
Politics of Honor

The Historical Aristotle

Despite profound differences in their conclusions, the most significant fact of Aristotle's life for an understanding of his political thought is that he was Plato's student. Indeed, he entered Plato's Academy at the age of eighteen and did not leave until Plato's death, twenty years later. He might have entertained hopes of replacing his mentor as head of the institution, but this position went to Plato's nephew. In any case, Aristotle left Athens for a period of over ten years, during which he pursued scholarship and served as a tutor, first at a Greek city-state on the coast of present-day Turkey and then at the court of Macedonia, where his pupil was the heir to the throne, later to be Alexander the Great.

Upon the murder of his father, Alexander became a king, and chose to conquer the world rather than continue his formal education. Aristotle returned to Athens just before Plato's nephew and successor died, and it is likely that he was seriously considered as a replacement. But once again the position went to someone else. Shortly thereafter, Aristotle established his own institution of higher learning, the Lyceum. There he taught and wrote for over a decade, and most of his extensive philosophical works, at least those that have survived, were produced for his students, rather than the general citizenry. In fact, of the two works most relevant to his political thought, the *Politics* and the *Nicomachean Ethics*, the first was probably compiled from lecture notes, and the second is a transcription of lectures by one of his disciples.

As one would expect, Aristotle's thought was strongly influenced by that of his long-time mentor. Yet a second significant fact of Aristotle's life serves to clarify a basic difference in their philosophical orientations. Insofar as the young Aristotle specialized in a particular subject of knowledge, it was not logic or mathematics but biology. This is probably what he taught before he left the Academy, and his initial investigations after he left were in this area. His father was a physician, and it may be that he initially intended to pursue a career in medicine himself. The importance of Aristotle's interest in biology lies in his refusal to make a sharp distinction, as did Plato, between logical analysis and sense perception. Even more important, Aristotle refused to believe that the reality of everyday experience was either senseless or a pale reflection of some more basic, higher reality. For him, there is a logic in reality, a logic that requires both careful observation and reasoning to discover.

A third fact of Aristotle's life, which might be related to his divergence from Plato in his estimate of the intrinsic value of political association, is that he was not a native Athenian but had adopted the city as his home. He was from a provincial Greek city that had lost its independence to Macedonia before his birth. Not only was he tutor to Alexander, his father was once court physician. Yet his familiarity with kings, empires, and aristocrats led to disdain rather than respect. Although almost as fearful of the leveling tendencies of democracy as Plato, he was even more concerned with the detrimental effects, both practical and moral, of an aristocratic monopoly on social and political honor. A regime dominated by middle-class citizens, rather than an aristocratic elite, was his ideal. Nonetheless, when Athens rebelled against Macedonian control at the death of Alexander in 323 B.C., Aristotle's adopted city drove him into exile because of his Macedonian connections. He died the following year, sixty-two years of age.

Human Nature and Rational Motivation

No function of man has so much permanence as virtuous activities. . . . The [virtuous] man will be happy throughout his life; for always . . . he will be engaged in virtuous action and contemplation, and he will bear the chances of life most nobly and altogether decorously. . . . The [virtuous] man can never become miserable.

—*Nichomachean Ethics*, bk. I, chap. 10

Ultimately, the motive of all action is happiness, and questions of rational ends and ethical behavior for Aristotle are questions of what leads to happiness. Of course, all sorts of amusements make us smile and have a good time, most of which we do not consider very important and some of which are positively dangerous to health. The question of rational motivation is not what will give momentary pleasure, but rather what will lead to a happy life. This in turn depends on our natural inclinations and needs; it depends, in other words, on human nature.

From Aristotle's perspective, to discern the nature of anything requires an understanding of its end or function. Although his analysis of the nature of reality varies considerably from the standpoint typically adopted in modern science, these metaphysical assumptions are as indispensable to his social and political thought as Plato's theory of ideas is to his. In brief, Aristotle presumed reality to be constituted by a finite number of "substances." A substance is something that does not change, irrespective of its changing relationships and altered attributes. For instance, a horse is a horse even when a fetus, and remains so throughout its lifetime, despite any changes, natural or accidental, in its appearance.

Recognizing substance is the starting point, not the goal, of knowledge; we cannot hope to understand why all substances exist. We can, however, discern both the uniqueness and pattern of development of a substance. For every substance is a mode of organization, or a "form," by which the matter or stuff of which it is composed at any particular time is ordered. A horse, of course, is composed of the same sort of stuff as trees, cliffs, and oceans. Its peculiar organization, not the matter of which it is composed, makes it a distinct thing.

An understanding of any substance depends on the discovery of its principles of development, the laws by which instances come into being and develop into completed or mature forms. To take Aristotle's own example, we would not truly comprehend an acorn until we understood four facts, or "causes," that allow us not only to describe it but also to see its inherent potential. First, there is the *material* cause, which is simply the mix of stuff composing the acorn. Second is the *formal* cause, the principles or laws through which the materials within the acorn and its environment are able to combine and grow, to realize the acorn's potential. Third, there must be an *efficient* cause, which means simply whatever brought these things together. Finally, and most significantly, there is the *final* cause, the mature form that defines a substance, toward which a thing moves as it develops. In the case of an acorn, obviously, the final cause is an oak tree.

Things, then, are defined by their natural potential. The principles through which they realize their potential, if unimpeded by defect or accident, are *natural laws*. The universe is a well-ordered place, where things move only with purpose. Although much of this motion is bound to appear random and senseless because we do not understand its final cause, painstaking observation and careful reasoning disclose the functional rationality everywhere in nature. The color of animals, for instance, can almost always be explained in terms of the need for camouflage or the facilitation of mating. Even the beauty of flowers is an invitation to bees and hummingbirds to harvest pollen and in the process to cross-fertilize the host plants. Everything has its purpose.

Yet accounting for things in terms of purpose, or "teleological" explanation, is no longer accepted in science, not even in biology. The color of plants and animals may be related to protection and procreation, but this is the result, by modern thinking, of the accidents of natural selection, rather than design. There are no substances in modern science. The physical and chemical laws of combination and change are universal, applying equally to the growth and death of both mammals and stars. No doubt they can be applied as well to human physiology, but they cannot as easily account for human psychology. We are purposeful, we have designs for ourselves and others. Only if there is an essential, identifying substance to humanity can our designs be objectively evaluated as appropriate or inappropriate to our essential nature. Without a soul, we would have neither purpose nor identity. We would be soulless.

What, then, is the identifying end of human beings, the fulfillment of which will lead to a happy life? It clearly cannot be physical reproduction, as it is for most life forms. For we are intelligent creatures, as much the product of our cultural priorities as our genetic inheritance; to reproduce, therefore, means much more than simple procreation. Similarly, we could never, as intelligent human beings, be satisfied with a succession of sensual pleasures and amusement. Not only are such things temporary, they are also trivial. Indeed, as Plato noted, if taken too seriously, they become destructive. Pleasure must be restrained to have more than a momentary existence. Consequently, the pursuit of pleasure must be subordinated to rational direction.

If rationality is the basis for self-sufficiency, then it may seem that Aristotle must be led, like Plato, to the conclusion that a life of inquiry and contemplation is the appropriate end of humanity. From Aristotle's perspective, however, a life of contemplation might be appropriate for gods, but not for human beings. There are two reasons for his refusal to follow his mentor. The first is simply that humans must devote a good deal of their time and effort to maintaining themselves and the social entities of which they are a part. Even the wealthiest misanthrope must attend to such mundane matters as bodily needs and the employment of those who handle his or her affairs. Moreover, only extraordinary good fortune will preserve the wealth and security of such a person.

More decisive is the second inherent limitation on a life of inquiry, and this is simply that it could not lead to a happy life because it would be too frustrating. Unlike Plato, Aristotle does not posit a realm of existence transcending the temporal reality of sense experience, accessible through disciplined, logical introspection. The order of the universe is immanent in daily life. Because this order is developmental, we cannot completely understand its movement without understanding the final cause toward which it moves. Consequently, our understanding of it must be partial and uncertain. Anyone devoting himself or herself completely to philosophy is doomed to a life of failure and frustration.

None of this should be taken to deny the joys of discovery or the need for human beings to have confidence in the rationality of their beliefs. Since the only way to gain such confidence is to develop the ability to articulate and defend beliefs, contemplation and inquiry are important dimensions of a happy life. But they are insufficient by themselves. Not only must we affirm the rationality of our beliefs, we must also act on them. Put differently, we must live up to our principles, applying them to the exigencies of experience. We must be active, and we must be rational. Principled activity, then, is the end most appropriate for human beings. For this reason, no one incapable of honorable action is considered a mature, or a complete, human being, irrespective of his or her age.

Will a life of honorable action necessarily be a happy life? History and literature offer innumerable instances of honorable people who have come to tragic ends, and most of us can think of despicable individuals who have been successful and prosperous. Yet success and prosperity are not the same as happiness, anymore than misfortune and failure preclude it. A happy life is not a continual state of bliss. Many of our most cherished moments are of trial and even danger. A happy life is one that would be lived again willingly. Unrelenting misfortune could very well render life unlivable, but it is more important that one be satisfied with oneself than with one's environment. If one is satisfied that the adversities of life were faced with honor, then one can face defeat and even destruction with self-respect. In contrast, one unable to be proud at the way life has been lived cannot die happy.

The Motivational Basis of Social Solidarity

The proof that the state is a creature of nature and prior to the individual is that the individual, when isolated, is not self-sufficing; and therefore he is like a part in relation to the whole. But he who is unable to live in society, or who has no need because he is sufficient for himself, must be either a beast or a god.

—*Politics*, bk. I, chap. 3

Happiness can be achieved only by living an honorable life, and an honorable life requires a community. More than any of the other great political thinkers discussed in this book, Aristotle stresses the dependence of humanity on society. We are all social creatures, and we could not truly forsake social membership without renouncing all hope of personal honor and humanity. Individuals have three inherent limitations impeding their human potential in the absence of social intercourse, all of which can be traced to the partial nature of human knowledge. In Aristotle's thought there are no self-sufficient philosophers who must be enticed to rule.

The first of these limitations is seen in the necessity to instill goodwill at an early age. Individual knowledge does not guarantee morality. In fact, it is quite common for people who know right from wrong to do wrong, either from weakness or maliciousness. Knowledge of morality is useless without the will and the ability to be good, and these are products of habit more than logical discourse. The disposition to be good probably originates in the emulation of parents, while the ability to be good is the result of training.

Most important in this regard is the instillation of a habitual distrust of extremes, either of excess or deficiency. In a world of functional interdependence a habit of moderation is essential if appropriate measures are to be applied, and even such virtues as honesty and loyalty can have negative consequences if blindly adhered to without regard to consequences. To act according to a principle requires the ability to discern which virtues are relevant, and to what degree. The only thing good in itself is nobility, or honorable action, and the moral virtues are only those facilities and dispositions instrumental to this end.

Yet even a well-trained person of good faith is unlikely consistently to embody ideals in action in the absence of like-minded associates. To be moral we need friends who can bolster our commitment to principle through their appreciation of honorable action and respect for those who engage in it. When moral conviction cannot be confirmed by logical demonstration, confirmation through mutual affirmation is necessary for most individuals. This requires, of course, that friends share the same moral convictions. But this is necessarily the case, for true friendship is possible only on the basis of common morality. It is true that people of diverse value orientations associate with one another for mutual benefit, and sometimes even enjoy one another's company just because of their differing perspectives. Yet personal associations resting on convenience or amusement do not qualify as true friendship because there is no mutual commitment, only considerations of private advantage. True friendship is a form of respect, even love. And the selfless love of another, paradoxically, is possible only for one who loves, or at least respects, oneself.

More exactly, selflessness means that one does not place oneself above another, that one judge another as an equal in the sense that one does not claim oneself to be more deserving or better. In Aristotle's use of the term, it would be inappropriate to say that a parent is a friend to the child. A parent may accept almost total responsibility for the welfare of the ward and be willing to make great personal sacrifices, but this primarily reflects a sense of duty and, secondarily, affection. The same sentiments, usually much diluted, apply to pets. Indeed, a parent is successful when the child matures into a person who can be accepted as a friend, who can be loved for what he or she is, rather than for the mere fact of a biological and biographical tie.

What kind of person one is depends on the criteria accepted to maintain one's self-respect. The basis of self-respect is the confidence that one has valid moral convictions that inform choice and guide action. To be equals and friends, individuals must consider one another to live by the same criteria by which each judges himself or herself. If one is truly what one purports to be, there simply is no rational basis to prefer oneself over the friend, since one loves the friend for exactly the same reason one respects oneself. In appreciation of the friend and enjoyment of the friend's companionship, the individual affirms the principles that make possible a life of honorable action.

The third and final limitation of the isolated individual is perhaps the most fundamental, in that it concerns the origins of the principles necessary for a happy life. Although principles must be considered objectively valid to serve their purpose, humans simply do not have the intellectual equipment to establish their ultimate moral priorities conclusively. We can assess degrees of both the logical incoherence and the practical difficulties of alternative moralities, but we cannot logically prove that any existing set of principles is the best possible. Consequently, we depend on society not only for the formation of our characters and sustaining friendships but also for the substantive moral priorities used to distinguish between honorable and dishonorable action. We can compare, evaluate, and even modify existing moralities. We cannot, however, create credible and practical moral systems by thought alone.

The Function and Organization of Authority

The laws are, and ought to be, relative to the constitution, and not the constitution to the laws. A constitution is the organization of offices in a state, and determines what is to be the governing body, and what is the end of each community. But laws are not to be confounded with the principles of the constitution.

—*Politics*, bk. IV, chap. 1

Rational social organization must serve human needs, and because humans have diverse needs, societies must be composed of more than one kind of social organization. Aristotle identifies three distinct levels of social organization, each necessary for a well-functioning society. Although their structure and tasks may vary with culture and technological development, each level of organization performs an essential, inescapable function in any society. The first of these three levels of organization is the household. The function of the household is to manage the necessities of individual existence, such as procreation, sleep, nourishment, and shelter.

In Aristotle's day the household produced many of the articles of personal consumption, but today production has been almost completely transferred to the second level of organization. This is what Aristotle identified as the "village," but what more modern theorists refer to as "civil society."

In essence, civil society is constituted by the market or contractual relations required for the specialized production and commercial distribution necessary in all but the most primitive of societies. In other words, civil society is the world of buying and selling, where individuals compete as well as cooperate in the pursuit of personal or household interest. As we see in the next section, a major source of political instability is the confusion of this second level of social organization with the third.

Whereas the first two levels of organization are concerned primarily with the use and acquisition of the necessities of life, the third is concerned with the good life. This highest level is the *polis,* or political community organized as a constitutional state. Whatever other tasks performed by the polis, and they will almost always include such important matters as the provision of security, the construction of public facilities, and the regulation of public ritual and morality, its essential function is the making of collective decisions. In a well-functioning polis, of course, citizens making collective decisions will be concerned above all with the public interest, and in the process they will be serving their own highest ends.

An individual's highest end is to live a happy life, which requires a life of honorable action. Without the support and recognition of a community it is extremely difficult to live such a life, and without the rights of citizenship it is impossible to reach its highest form, a life of noble action. In fact, the duties of citizenship create an arena for noble action, where individuals can publicly act in accordance with their values and mutually honor exceptional valor and ingenuity in the service of common ideals.

Citizenship is akin to friendship, a relationship of equality based on the ability to live up to a common standard. Consequently, citizenship requires common standards, or shared ideals, and this is the most fundamental aspect of the constitution that defines a polis. A constitution, then, is more than a stipulation of public offices, political powers, and procedures for governing. It is also the internalized values and expectations that are sometimes called political culture. Constitutional principles are the identifying core of any political community worthy of the name.

Correspondingly, the primary duty of a citizen is to preserve the integrity of constitutional values by supporting institutions and policies that serve the needs of the community and embody its principles. The nature of the institutions will vary with both the particular principles of the constitution and the particular environment within which the political community must subsist. The most important question of organization is the determination of who can be a citizen and who cannot. This, too, will vary with circumstance. In general, however, the citizen must not only have internalized as personal priorities the basic constitutional principles that define the polis but also have the training and character to act responsibly, in conformity with these collective values.

Since citizenship, like friendship, is a relation of equality, citizens must share in the making of collective decisions. Ideally, there is no basis for some of them to claim more power than the others. This is why Aristotle defines citizens as those who know both how to rule and how to obey. Those who know only how to obey, no matter how important the services they may render to their societies, can only be loyal subjects, not true citizens. Moreover, those who might qualify as citizens in one polis may only be fit to be subjects in another. The practical problems and moral ambiguities facing the notables of a band of hunter-gatherers, for example, are likely to be much less intricate and require less sophistication than those facing the authorities of a complex nation-state.

In any event, the primary purpose of political association is thoroughly ethical; through citizenship, individuals protect and apply the common values that define the polis, and in the process reaffirm and amplify their own moral commitments. The fulfillment of this ethical purpose is not just morally good but is essential for the stability and even the survival of the state. Regimes not based on a common set of values are, at best, no more than alliances or, at worst, little more than prison camps. In either instance, only utility or fear makes collective action possible. Just as we cannot rely on those whose friendship is based on considerations of personal advantage, regimes uncommitted to common moral principles cannot trust those they supposedly serve.

Aristotle's General Theory of Political Change and Stability

... we must remember that good laws, if they are not obeyed, do not constitute good government. Hence there are two parts of good government: one is the actual obedience of citizens to the laws, the other part is the goodness of the laws which they obey.

—*Politics*, bk. IV, chap. 8

All living substances change. In Aristotle's view of the nature of things, they either grow or decay. Things grow when they are realizing their natural potential and begin to decay when they cease to do so. This is as true of human beings as oak trees, and it is also true of political communities. The "efficient" causes of political change are too varied to consider here, but the "material" and "formal" causes are everywhere the same. The former are simply the stakes of public affairs, which can always be reduced to either honor, in the case of real political communities, or profit, in the case of perverted ones. The formal cause is invariably a sense of justice or injustice, which controls the extent to which the allocation of honor or profit is considered acceptable.

Perverted regimes are those in which the rulers do not rule for the good of the entire society but in their own interest. As previously indicated, these regimes are really no more than alliances because they are not based on common principles. To be sure, the rulers justify their rule in terms of fairness, and no doubt they are usually sincere in this conviction. But whether one thinks a given distribution of benefits is "fair" depends entirely on the yardstick used to measure it. In perverted regimes, this depends largely on how such a yardstick applies to oneself. As Aristotle put it, when the wealthy rule, they believe that because subjects differ on one dimension, wealth, they should differ by a similar ratio on other social privileges, especially political power. Conversely, when the poor rule, they justify their power with the assertion that equality in one thing, typically the mere status of citizenship, should lead to equality in all.

Irrespective of whether the wealthy few rule, which Aristotle called "oligarchy," or the many poor, identified by Aristotle as "democracy," perverted regimes are necessarily unstable because of internal conflict. Indeed, an emphasis on "distributive justice," a fair distribution of policy benefits, ensures that individuals will approach public affairs with a concern for personal advantage, rather than a concern for the public good. Since the populations of all but the most primitive societies are divided into distinct economic groups, and almost all societies have both rich and poor, the inevitable result of an excessive concern with distributive justice is class conflict. Politics in these regimes is, to use contemporary terminology, zero sum; there are no winners without losers. And when a portion of society loses consistently, there is no dishonor in treason, for politics in these regimes has nothing to do with honor.

Justice requires that equals be treated equally, but the only criterion of equality appropriate to a genuine political community is measured in terms of honor. In effect, the prevalence of distributive justice indicates confusion of the polis with civil society, the second level of social organization. In real political communities political distinctions are based upon merit, rather than numerical formulas. Merit in turn is assessed on the basis of the ability to contribute to the public good, and the public good is defined ultimately by the constitutional principles that make the community and citizenship possible.

In "aristocracies" only those most capable of articulating and acting on constitutional principles are eligible for citizenship. Most of the population, however much they may personally affirm collective values and be ready to support the regime, lack sufficient education and resources for public service. Those forced by necessity to toil at a trade or devote themselves in some other way to serving at the pleasure of others are not likely to have had either the leisure or the experience of responsibility to develop the knowledge and skill to participate effectively in the leadership of the community. This, of course, is a matter of degree, but politics in aristocracies is the business of cultural elites who have been educated for statesmanship. Consequently, all things being equal, public discourse will be conducted on a relatively high level, and stringent standards of ability and integrity will be applied.

Aristocracies have the advantage of requiring those capable of meeting high standards to be as good as they can be and in the process to lead a highly honorable existence. Yet they suffer from two defects that, under most circumstances, render aristocracy a less than desirable form of government. First, they make individuals as good as they can be by refusing to make as many individuals as possible good. By restricting citizenship to the very best, all those who might have the ability to participate at a somewhat lower level are denied the opportunity both to develop their potential and to have lives aspiring to nobility. In an aristocracy, most are relegated to an audience.

There is little reason to believe, however, that everyone in the audience will be satisfied with cheering from the sidelines, and this constitutes a second, more practical defect of aristocracies. A system of good laws is worthless unless the laws are actually obeyed. Although a well-functioning aristocracy, by definition, would serve the interests of the whole according to common standards, it is very difficult to keep those excluded from public decisions convinced of this. Aristocracies, therefore, are inherently unstable.

Consequently, if conditions allow, a more popular form of government is to be preferred. Aristotle calls the best practical form a "polity," and describes it as a mixture of aristocratic and democratic elements. It is democratic, not in the sense of rule by the poor, but because the rights of citizenship are extended to all who affirm community values and can contribute to their realization. The standards should not be set so high as to exclude a high percentage of the population. A polity is aristocratic to the extent that less privileged citizens are either discouraged from exercising their rights to participate in public decisions or encouraged to defer to the more experienced and capable. The election of representatives, as opposed to direct popular votes, or the lack of compensation for public service are examples of aristocratic practices in popular regimes.

Well-functioning polities have a number of important advantages over aristocracies. The first is the moral advantage of allowing a larger number of individuals to enjoy the happiness of an honorable life. The second, increased stability, naturally follows from the first. On one level, there will be less resentment at being excluded from participation in the affairs of one's community. On a deeper, more positive level, citizens will have a stake in the protection of the constitution and be more inclined to sacrifice short-term personal advantages in order to further common goals. Buttressed by the mutual esteem of fellow citizens, self respect will increasingly rest on one's status as a responsible citizen, and one will act accordingly.

The cost of these advantages, of course, is a level of political deliberation less sophisticated than would be the case with more stringent qualifications for participation. By itself, this could be expected to result in less rigorous standards of honor, as well as less intelligent collective decisions. These negative results are likely to be greatly reduced, however, if not completely negated, by the fact that a polity is a mixed system. Almost all have the right to participate in public affairs, but not all will participate equally. Most of those without the leisure or training for effective participation will look on the duties of citizenship as a burdensome distraction from vocational endeavors. They will be only too willing to defer to those with the desire for public responsibility and the capacity for political leadership. Indeed, the same individuals who would be the only citizens in an aristocracy are apt to be most influential citizens in a polity.

Whatever the remaining disadvantages for effective public policy, they are more than counterbalanced by the greatest of all the benefits made possible by a polity. Politics in a polity serves to educate the mass of citizens. Leaders, in this mixed system, must gain the support of their less active peers. Deference to superior ability will not be automatic; they must explain, exhort, and, most important, set a good example. In the process, they will be tutoring their fellow citizens, and over time the sophistication of political discourse will tend to increase as a result. With greater sophistication comes heightened confidence, and confidence increases the incidence of responsible participation.

Not only does political discourse in a polity tend to educate the populace for higher levels of citizenship, it also tends to refine and enrich the constitutional values that define the community. The more people are forced to explain constitutional principles to one another and rationalize their application to unprecedented circumstances, the more logically coherent and comprehensive these principles become. Citizens increasingly see their principles as functionally rational, rather than simply as a set of traditional prescriptions. In fact, traditional cultural interpretations are slowly altered as they are purged of rigid taboos exposed by experience as serving no purpose. In Aristotle's view of the nature of things, the truth is always functional, and the genuinely functional is always true.

A polity, then, is a vehicle for constitutional and moral progress. An aristocracy, in contrast, is an inherently static form of government. This is the real, underlying source of its instability. Not only are opportunities for individual growth and development stifled for most members of society, even the personal growth of the aristocratic citizen is necessarily inhibited. For the primary concern of a well-functioning aristocracy must be the maintenance of the high qualifications of its citizens. Since constitutional principles serve as the standards by which qualifications are assessed, aristocracies cannot permit open discussion of alternative interpretations of these principles and therefore foreclose any possibility that they might be improved through adaptation and extension. Aristocracy cannot grow because an artificial perfection is sought at a less than optimal level, and in the process the slow, spontaneous progress inherent in the nature of things is arrested.

Natural progress is spontaneous, rather than planned. The rationality of things is revealed slowly, through experience and diligent observation. The slow advance of civilization can be distorted by the accidents of history, but because the wisdom of experience is cumulative, it cannot for long be impeded. Just as the political community is the basis of individual morality and happiness, so too is it the vehicle for the improvement of humanity. Consequently, progress is best served, not by the conscious effort to improve, but by the commitment to preserve one's cultural heritage, adapting it to new conditions only out of necessity. Because the paramount duty of all true citizens is to protect the constitution that defines the community, the open politics of a well-functioning polity is more conservative than reformist. On collective commitment to common values rests the resilience of a regime, and on the need to explore their meaning lies its ability to adapt and grow.

The Politics of Honor

Like Plato, Aristotle requires that citizens and subjects have faith in the existence of an immutable truth. Unlike his mentor, however, he does not think it wise to presume that any mortal can fully comprehend the mysteries of existence. Instead, we must have faith that there is reason in history, that events happen for a purpose. The evolution of civilization is not aimless but is the story of rational progress. Consequently, we can have faith that our own institutional and moral principles are the product of rational adaptation to the unfolding order of the universe and therefore entail an objective moral truth.

Beyond this faith in the rationality of communal principles, we must also have faith in one another. In the absence of philosopher kings, citizens must take responsibility for protecting the integrity of constitutional values and adapting them to the demands of the day. This is the primary end of politics. For this reason, those who lack either the inclination or the ability to pursue the public good effectively must be either discouraged from exercising the rights of citizenship or excluded from citizenship altogether. At a minimum, in a well-ordered polity citizens must be able to recognize and honor acts of public service.

A Brief Guide to the Literature

As with Plato, we are unlikely ever to have a useful biography of Aristotle. There are, however, many attempts to give an overview of the man's thought. Since Aristotle not only delved into the fundamental philosophical questions of existence and knowing but also systematically explored their implications in such diverse realms as science, art, and politics, this is not an easy task. One of the most successful of these attempts, notable for brevity and readability as well as insight, is A.E. Taylor, *Aristotle* (1955). Two more lengthy and difficult books are also worth consulting, Werner Jaeger's *Aristotle: Fundamentals of the History of His Development* (1948), and Marjorie Grene's *A Portrait of Aristotle* (1963).

Jaeger attempts a sort of intellectual biography based almost solely on analysis of Aristotle's writings. Grene is highly critical of this developmental approach to making sense of Aristotle and argues that his philosophical works display a systematic unity having its foundations in his biological investigations.

Sir Ernest Barker's *The Political Thought of Plato and Aristotle* (1959) comes close to being the standard survey of Aristotle's social and political thought. A more controversial analysis is presented by Leo Strauss in *The City and Man* (1964); Strauss maintains that Aristotle, like Plato, affirmed the superiority of the philosophical life over engagement in public affairs. By this account, Aristotle's political thought ultimately was intended to make the world safe for philosophy, rather than extol the blessings of citizenship. A similar, but somewhat moderated position informs Carnes Lord's *Education and Culture in the Political Thought of Aristotle* (1982).

This issue of the relative importance of citizenship plays an important role in another, the status of women. Both Susan Moller Okin, in *Women in Western Political Thought* (1979), and Jean Bethke Elshtain, in *Public Man, Private Woman: Women in Social and Political Thought* (1981), have argued that Aristotle's apparent view of women as inferior beings follows from their exclusion from public affairs. If the best life is a life of noble action, achieved in the public sphere, then those whose natures consign them to the essentially private spheres of the household or economic activity, such as women and slaves, can never attain human excellence. As part of her critique of these views Judith A. Swanson, in *The Public and the Private in Aristotle's Political Philosophy* (1992), maintains that Aristotle did not elevate the public sphere above the private, that each is a necessary and equal complement to the other. Bernard Yack, in *The Problems of a Political Animal: Community, Justice, and Conflict in Aristotelian Political Thought* (1993), is even more sweeping in his attempt to argue that previous commentators have overestimated the intrinsic value of community and citizenship in Aristotle's thought.

Even though many consider Aristotle to be the first political scientist, an Aristotelian social science is based on assumptions of natural order and the social functionality of tradition that most advocates of modern social science have found questionable. The divergence is clearly evident in Larry Arnhart's claim, in *Aristotle on Political Reasoning: A Commentary on the "Rhetoric"* (1981), that political rhetoric is a rational form of discourse appropriate for politics and political science alike. For an engaging case for the superiority of an Aristotelian approach to social science, see Stephen G. Salkever, *Finding the Mean: Theory and Practice in Aristotelian Political Philosophy* (1990). Finally, Roger D. Masters's biological interpretation of political life, *The Nature of Politics* (1989), is self-consciously Aristotelian.

St. Augustine and the Politics of Sin

The Historical St. Augustine

At his death in 430 A.D., St. Augustine had been bishop of the northern African city of Hippo for thirty-five years. When he first assumed this responsibility, Christians were a minority in this important port on the Mediterranean Sea, and the authority of the church was undermined by bitter theological disputes. At the end of his life, Hippo and the rest of the Roman Empire were mostly Christian, and the church had imposed an orthodox doctrine on its clergy. The consolidation of Christianity during this period was the result of a number of impersonal forces. The forging of doctrinal unity, in contrast, owed much to Augustine's intellect, his polemical skill, and even his willingness to persecute his rivals ruthlessly. Yet, as he lay dying, Hippo was under siege by one of the barbarian tribes that inundated and eventually destroyed the Roman Empire. Although Augustine personally considered Rome's decline a disaster, his influence on subsequent generations did much to erode classical learning in the Christian world of medieval Europe.

St. Augustine was himself thoroughly steeped in the literature and philosophy of Greece and Rome. Northern Africa was at that time a fertile agricultural region and an economically important part of the Roman Empire. Born in 354 in a small city inland from Hippo, Augustine was a Latin-speaking Roman citizen. His father, a person of humble means, had great ambitions for him and was able with the help of a patron to provide his son with an extensive education aimed at a career in law and public service. His mother Monica, an uneducated Christian, was more concerned with his spiritual disposition than his worldly success, and in the long run her influence was more decisive than all the great authors of classical civilization.

Her victory, although complete, came late. As related in the *Confessions,* his autobiographical prayer, Augustine rejected the faith of his mother and sought to find the meaning of life in more intellectually sophisticated alternatives. He turned first to Manichaeism. The devotees of this religion interpreted all existence as a struggle between two natural forces, those of light and those of darkness, and claimed the ability to demonstrate the truth of this proposition to all who would listen. After several years, Augustine realized that such a claim was false. He became a Platonist, attempting to find a foundation for life in the immutable verities of abstract ideas, seeing all existence as emanating from some absolute good.

Yet Augustine eventually came to see that neither he nor any other mortal could ever really know absolute good, and this set the stage for his conversion to Christianity. Faith was inevitable. For all their intellectual accomplishments, the great thinkers of the ancient world had utterly failed to demonstrate the nature of good and the meaning of life. For all their pretensions, they offered nothing but transitory goals and, at best, a fleeting happiness helpless in the face of human mortality. Augustine accepted his mother's faith, gave up a successful career as a professor in the Roman capital of Milan, and returned to Africa to devote himself to God.

In 410, the city of Rome was sacked for the first time by a barbarian army, and a large number of Roman notables sought refuge in the African provinces. This traumatic event resulted in some hostility toward the church. Many of these influential refugees were intellectually sophisticated individuals who believed Christianity to be little more than a fabric of superstitions, and some now claimed that its elevation to the state religion threatened to undermine the classical civilization and virtues that had made Rome great. The dominant status of the church seemed to be in jeopardy.

To meet this challenge, Augustine wrote his greatest work, *The City of God.* Everyone must make a fundamental choice, he argued, between God and earthly happiness. Those who choose God, to be citizens only in Heaven, at least can hope for salvation. Those who choose to be citizens of an earthly city, however, must suffer the destruction that is the fate of all earthly things. If Rome was great, it was only because this served God's purposes, not because of the supposed virtues of classical civilization. Augustine resorted to his vast erudition to expose the philosophical and moral poverty of human knowledge and culture. Even Plato, he wrote, does not compare "to any faithful Christian man."

Human Nature and Rational Motivation

... when the will abandons what is above itself, and turns to
what is lower, it becomes evil—not because that is evil to
which it turns, but because the turning itself is wicked.

—*The City of God,* bk. XII

In Augustine's eyes, Plato's great strength was also his fatal weakness. This greatest of philosophers was able to demonstrate that all existence and beauty must emanate from a single source, but he erred in presuming to be able to apprehend this essence of existence. Plato not only believed reality to be rational but also that at least some humans were capable of understanding its very nature. Yet this is a futile hope, as well as a sacrilege. For the source of all existence is God, and no mortal can ever hope to equal God's understanding. Reality is indeed rational, for it conforms to God's purpose. Yet our understanding of things must remain relative and incomplete because we are not God.

Human reason is a frail and uncertain thing, and those who define humanity in terms of rationality do so under the illusion that reason can make us self-sufficient. They believe, in other words, that we are capable of deriving rational rules by which we can live meaningful, happy lives. Yet since God is the maker of all things, nothing can be sufficient in itself without Him. What exists does so only to the extent to which it serves God's purpose. Insofar as we deny God, we inevitably undermine the basis of our own existence and destroy ourselves. God did not create us to be independent of Him, and our reason allows us neither to control our fate nor even to accommodate ourselves to it.

Our fate is death. As mortals, we cannot escape this fact, and by ourselves we cannot accede to it. For life without God is without value. A happy life is a delusion. Pain, sorrow, disappointment, and fear are the inexorable accompaniments to pleasure, joy, hope, and comfort. With love comes the grief of separation if not betrayal, and fame is a meaningless illusion. For everything human is small and temporary. Our buildings, our roads, our art, our monuments, and even our history will be eradicated and forgotten in the passage of time. Life on earth can be nothing more than a melange of affliction and relief, which finally ends in death.

God did not create us to be self-sufficient, and He did not create us to deny Him. He did, however, give us a choice, and this ability to choose is our distinguishing trait. God made us in His own image. This does not mean that He gave us His understanding, for that would make us His equal. Instead, He gave us *will,* the ability and freedom to choose. Our reason is a weak thing, which does not determine our will but is itself determined by will. In other words, what we think about things depends on the attitude we take toward them, rather than vice versa.

Although we are defined by will, our range of genuine choice is actually quite limited. Since we cannot understand the nature of things, we cannot control them. Indeed, we cannot even completely understand and control ourselves, a point to which I later return. For the moment, I want to stress that from Augustine's perspective, we have only one genuine choice to make, and we cannot rely on reason to make it. This is the choice between God and ourselves, whether we will devote our lives to God or to earthly happiness. Reason cannot make this choice. Our love of God cannot be based on reason, for we are incapable of comprehending God. Instead, the choice must be based on faith. You either will God or you will yourself.

A choice must be made. Either you believe the meaning of life can be found only in God or you believe it possible to find meaning and happiness on earth. There are no alternatives, and there are no agnostics. In matters of faith, to doubt is to deny. To say you will believe in God only if His existence can be demonstrated or proved is nothing more than personal conceit. You have already made your choice. Indeed, in the last analysis sin is nothing more than pride, for pride is self-love and therefore a denial of God. God gave us the will to affirm or deny Him, and when we choose ourselves rather than Him, we sin. We, through our own will, are the creators of sin. God is the source of all good; we are the source of all evil.

Through his critique of classical philosophy, Augustine attempted to demonstrate the futility of all efforts to live according to human reason. At the core of every secular ethic is a completely arbitrary, willful claim to have discovered the criterion of human fulfillment. Yet the lover of God is no more able to demonstrate the validity of his or her commitment than the lover of self. One lives by faith, the other by foolish presumption. The lover of God hopes for salvation, while the lover of self anticipates success and happiness. Neither commitment can be philosophically rationalized. Only a lover of God, however, can really acknowledge and live with this fact.

How does a lover of God live? What must be done to achieve salvation? The seemingly obvious answer is simply to refrain from sin, to avoid pride and maintain one's commitment to God. Yet there are two complications that render this simple answer completely inadequate. The first derives from the fact that God placed us on earth to live, and in the course of daily life we are constantly exposed to earthly temptations. To live requires a degree of aspiration and success. We must eat, make love, raise families, and earn a livelihood. Who has not enjoyed an especially good meal, pined after a particularly attractive mate, boasted of the accomplishments of children, or known personal ambition? Everyday existence is a conspiracy of temptation because any form of success is a potential source of pride. In fact, the belief that one has avoided such temptation is itself an insidious source of pride.

The second complication is even more treacherous. Temptation is everywhere, and yet our ability to resist is limited. Just as we cannot understand and control our environment, so too we cannot understand and control ourselves. We can divide humanity into those who love God and those who love self, but we cannot separate sinners and saints. For we are all sinners. Not only is it difficult to avoid feeling some degree of pride at worldly success, even rejected temptations are accompanied by secret desires. Sin is not the result of evil deeds but is created by deviant will that may or may not result in overt behavior. Our most sincere intent to devote ourselves to God is undermined by our biology and our secret, perhaps only semiconscious, passions. Human beings are inherently sinners. In the last analysis, salvation depends on God's grace.

Consequently, the genuine lover of God must not only attempt to resist pride and the other pleasures of earthly existence but also must recognize the daily failures in this lifelong effort and beg for God's forgiveness. Anyone not feeling the need for God's forgiveness is lost. The primary duty of the Christian is to confess one's sins to oneself, acknowledge them to God, and pray for absolution. Our faith tells us that God, as the source of all good, surely wants us to make the right choice. But He has given us will, and the choice is ours to make. So we are able to make the correct choice, to will it, even though we are unable to give complete effect to this choice in thought and action. For the choice to remain genuine, we must identify our deviations and see them as sins against God. Because we sin, we are unworthy of grace. But certainly we can hope that the God of our faith, the source of all good, will forgive us if we genuinely struggle with our mortal defects. The Christian lives by hope derived from faith, according to an ethic of humility, asceticism, and selfless acceptance of duty.

The Motivational Basis of Social Solidarity

... this heavenly city ... while it sojourns on earth, calls citizens out of all nations, and gathers together a society of pilgrims of all languages, not scrupling about diversities in the manners, laws, and institutions whereby earthly peace is secured and maintained, but recognizing, however various they are, they all tend to one and the same end of earthly peace.

—*The City of God*, bk. XIX

Obviously, the primary concerns of a Christian are with one's personal orientation toward God and self. Nonetheless, the Christian cannot withdraw into a private world, refusing to be concerned with worldly affairs. God placed us on this earth, and we have no right to ignore this fact. Just because we must spend our lives attempting to resist earthly temptations does not mean that we can reject our earthly existence. To do so would be sinful. It would be a repudiation of God's Will, a refusal to play our designated part in His grand design. Genuine faith in God does not allow one to become a hermit anymore than it allows one to commit suicide.

We must be residents of earth, but we must not be citizens of earth. If we are to have any hope of receiving God's grace, we must look on ourselves as simply traveling through a strange and terrible place. In other words, we must consider ourselves as no more than pilgrims, seeking a holy place that no mortal has ever seen. Only our faith that such a place exists allows us to continue our journey. If faith falters, the loneliness of the road inevitably will compel us to abandon the pilgrimage, to attempt to find a home somewhere along the way. Only those who define themselves by their faith as citizens of the City of God, rather than of any earthly city, have any hope of salvation. In this world we must be aliens.

Nevertheless, aliens are residents, and as such they share many of the same needs as those who have chosen to be citizens of some earthly city. Irrespective of whether one is just passing through or considers it home, to live on earth requires the ability to provide for daily necessities, as well as a measure of security. Like the local residents, Christians will be productive and law-abiding, and will even be willing to cooperate with the natives in mutually beneficial, practical pursuits. In fact, citizens of the world are likely to find it particularly advantageous to cooperate with Christians because the latter are such practical, reliable people. Trustworthy because they have no use for luxuries, accommodating because they care not for honors or other forms of personal distinction, Christians are much more a resource than a threat to the citizens of earthly cities.

For the same reasons, Christians would rather deal with one another than those who have not chosen God. However, the sojourners of faith have more important reasons to band together, and wherever there are Christians there will be a church. Because Christians live by faith, they need the support of one another if they are not to stray from the path. The church itself is an earthly institution that serves an earthly function; it must not be confused with the City of God, which is defined as the community of the faithful, regardless of whether on Earth or in Heaven. The primary purpose of the church is to reinforce the faith of its members by expounding on the word of God and exposing the nature and ubiquity of sin.

Yet there is another function for the church, corresponding to a duty shared by all Christians. The Christian pilgrim does not fulfill his or her duty simply by steadfastly continuing the pilgrimage. There is another worldly goal for the Christian, beyond resistance to temptation and confession of sin. Although we cannot pretend to know God's plan, our faith tells us that He wants us to choose correctly and that He has given us Christ as well as His word to help us in this choice. For these reasons, we can be confident that He wants us to devote ourselves to the propagation of His word, to help others understand the possibility of salvation though faith. The pilgrim is only passing through, and must deal with local residents to acquire the provisions for the journey. But the pilgrim cannot leave it at that, having no more to do with them than practically required. Instead, the pilgrimage must be explained to them, and they must be invited to join the journey.

The church, therefore, must do more than simply articulate the word of God and tend to the pastoral needs of its flock; it must also propagate the faith. Every Christian church is a mission, especially in societies where a significant proportion of the population does not profess the faith. The community of the faithful must be concerned not just with their own souls but also with those of their faithless neighbors. Christianity is not an inward-looking sect, taking no interest in worldly affairs beyond those necessary to ensure its own survival. A life based on faith requires a commitment to the well-being even of those who have not yet seen the futility of all other paths. True lovers of God are obligated to do God's work on earth.

The Function and Organization
of Authority

... earthly kingdoms are given by Him both to the good and
the bad; lest His worshippers, still under the conduct of a very
weak mind, should covet these gifts from Him as some great
things.

—*The City of God,* bk. IV

Doing God's work on earth can mean no more than loving God,
begging His forgiveness, and propagating His word. Mere mortals must
live by faith, since the understanding of God's purpose is beyond the
power of human reason. Consequently, none can claim to act in His
name. Having rejected all secular ends other than mere survival, and
limited religious goals to piety and preaching, Augustine provides no
basis for a specifically Christian commonwealth, or even a basis for a
Christian political ethic. There may be Christian politicians, but their
politics will be distinguished only by their deference to the Christian
church, not by their methods or their adherence to a certain sort of constitutional structure.

In the last analysis, all political power rests on brute force. Try as
they might, political philosophers will never be able to ascertain rational
principles of political justice. Since human beings are not self-sufficient,
the principles they formulate to bring themselves happiness and harmo-
nize their relationships are bound to be defective. Such rules inevitably
rest on arbitrary assertions that some particular thing or condition will
make our lives meaningful and happy. Whatever this thing or condition
is purported to be, its possession and enjoyment can only be temporary,
and it can never give us self-understanding or save us from our ultimate
fate as mortals, decline and death.

Moreover, for two distinct reasons, principles of justice cannot provide the basis of political order. The first reason is that such principles
are derived from arbitrary premises. Not only is the supposed benefit inadequate, the mere fact that its status as the ultimate good rests on
nothing but assertion guarantees that many will refuse to accept it.
Only force can establish the semblance of consensus on the operative
principles of justice. The second reason is even more fundamental.
Those who search for justice on earth have chosen to be citizens of an
earthly city; they have, in effect, rejected God and chosen themselves.
They may sincerely espouse their love of justice, of humanity, or of

country, but in the last analysis this is all pride. Many are willing to sacrifice to advance their worldly values, but few are willing to humble or humiliate themselves. Pride is inherent in the search for worldly justice and will always be a source of competition and political strife.

Despite the ideological pretensions typical of governmental authorities, political power can never be based on some notion of justice. Even a state committed to true justice, dedicated to the devotion to God as the source of all good, must ultimately rest on a preponderance of coercive power. Human beings are congenital sinners lacking the willpower consistently to live up to their obligations, which is why even Christians must depend on the grace of God. Just for this reason, political authority serves a constructive purpose, and Christians will under most conditions be faithful and supportive subjects. Indeed, they will be good subjects even in regimes making no pretense of serving any conception of justice, let alone claiming devotion to God. They will be so, not from any love of authority, but from a purely pragmatic assessment of the conditions of earthly existence.

Everyone seeks peace, but those who choose to be citizens of a worldly city cannot achieve it. For they believe that a just peace could be established on earth, that personal meaning and social harmony can be realized if only the proper principles or customs are observed. Because they believe in the possibility of an earthly peace, they will war against all enemies of their particular creed and may even withdraw support from their own leaders when the presumed benefits of citizenship are not forthcoming. Paradoxically, the belief in the possibility of a perfect earthly peace, which follows from the belief in human self-sufficiency, leads inevitably to war.

Christians, in contrast, believe that peace on earth is, at best, partial and temporary. Perfect peace can be attained only through God's grace in Heaven. Imperfect as earthly peace may be, however, it is useful. Pilgrims, like all who travel through strange lands, place a high premium on order and stability. If unprovoked, they have almost no reason to engage in sedition. For these citizens of the City of God, mere denial of the rights of citizenship in an earthly city can mean nothing in itself. Even oppression and exploitation are insufficient grounds for disobedience to whatever political authority holds sway. Indeed, there are distinct advantages for the Christian in political subjugation in that the oppressed and deprived are likely to be faced with fewer earthly temptations. All things being equal, Christians will accept the rules and regulations imposed on them and will fulfill the civic duties stipulated by any established authority.

There is only one requirement that must be met before a government is entitled to receive the support of Christians. Beyond a code of conduct required by the word of God, Christians have no earthly aspirations, which is why they cannot have political ideals. They do have, however, a few inescapable earthly tasks. These place distinct conditions on their willingness to support particular governments, and especially their willingness to tolerate rule by non-Christians. Specifically, Christians must be allowed to worship God. They also must be allowed to spread the word of God. Together, these conditions add up to the requirement that political authority must not oppose the creation of a church or significantly curtail its proselytizing activity. In short, citizens of the City of God will be obedient subjects of earthly cities as long as the latter refrain from persecuting or unduly inhibiting the Christian church.

Obviously, all things being equal, it would be preferable to have political power wielded by Christians, rather than the faithless. Not only would this minimize the chances of persecution, but also under most circumstances the active cooperation of those who control the police function of the state is likely to aid the church's efforts to spread the word of God. Yet there are dangers peculiar to rule by Christians. Although Christian rulers are highly unlikely to persecute their fellow believers, there is always the threat that political authorities will use their power to dominate, rather than serve, the church. Irrespective of the effects on its proselytizing efforts, the domination of the church by politicians would inevitably undermine its most important functions: to help sinners resist earthly temptations, acknowledge failure to do so, and sincerely beg for God's forgiveness.

Political rulers cannot be spiritual leaders. Their task is to create a degree of order through domination. To create an imperfect, always precarious earthly peace requires that rulers be primarily occupied with earthly things. It also requires that they deal with potential threats to public order in a manner not completely in accord with how good Christians would like to act. Indeed, a good Christian would not want to rule and would do so only out of a sense of duty. Yet who could be more subject to earthly temptation than those who exercise secular power? Even more than the typical sinner, rulers will have a personal need for the church, for they invariably will have much to confess. Whatever political institutions are found effective in particular circumstances, it is imperative for both the rulers and the church that the former defer to the latter in all things concerning the faith.

St. Augustine's General Theory of Political Change and Stability

... the peace of the unjust man is not worthy to be called peace in comparison with the peace of the just. And yet what is perverted must of necessity be in harmony with, and in dependence on, and in some part of the order of things, for otherwise it would have no existence at all.

—*The City of God,* bk. XIX

From Augustine's perspective, the existence of even a degree of political order is much more problematic than the persistence of political instability. Instability has deep, ineradicable roots in human nature. From pride stems ambition, envy, and contentiousness. From presumed self-sufficiency comes dissatisfaction with all dependence, and eventual frustration with the failure of all efforts to evade it. Such efforts are inevitably futile, both because pride undermines cooperation and, more fundamentally, because fate is controlled by God. When humans attempt to control their own fate, this is no more than foolish pride. To deny dependence on God, to turn toward ourselves rather than Him, is to will our own destruction. To turn away from God is to deny the source of all being; it is a turn toward decay and death.

How, then, is it possible for political communities to grow and prosper, even temporarily? And more specifically, how was it possible for the Roman Empire, built on pagan foundations, to steadily expand its power until it had almost encompassed the known world? Augustine's answer to the more general question is based on an essential condition of all collective endeavor, which is simply a common love sufficiently powerful to hold in abeyance love of self. Even criminal gangs must be based on more than simple greed if they are to avoid self-destruction through mistrust.

Criminal gangs can be expected to be relatively unstable, however, because honor among thieves is bound to be rather weak. When disloyalty is profitable, mutual appreciation of daring or cleverness will provide criminal associates with little security from one another. This, no doubt, is why more successful criminal organizations typically attempt to be "families" to their members, and many have actually been families. More conventional political associations rely on more idealistic appeals, such as the "people," the "nation," or some principle of justice and morality. As long as individuals rest their sense of self-esteem on these arbitrary fabrications, they will be willing to make the sacrifices necessary for collective action.

Nonetheless, to the extent this willingness to sacrifice is derived from self-esteem, it provides an inherently unreliable basis for common endeavor and political stability. Self-esteem is just another name for self-love, and the mere fact that individuals love themselves for the same reason does not change the fact that they love themselves rather than one another. Sooner or later, but inevitably, human pride will undermine the bonds that hold us together. A common love can hold the effects of self-love in abeyance, but it cannot eliminate them. Only a Christian community, based on a common love of God and a denial of self, could have any hope of avoiding the personal competitiveness that is the inescapable result of pride.

How, then, did Rome overcome the effects of its godlessness? Augustine gives two answers. The first refers to the peculiar emphasis that Roman culture placed on public honor and glory. Roman citizens were more willing to sacrifice for the interests of the state than others because, given their attachment to public recognition as meaningful in itself, the rewards were relatively greater. This answer, however, is inadequate. The Roman citizen's insatiable desire for public acclaim was often detrimental to success and stability. As Augustine pointed out at great length in *The City of God,* the desire for office and public prestige was as much the source of ruthless ambition and incredible corruption as heroic self-sacrifice. Other communities shared the Roman love of public esteem, and Rome was too great for too long for such an analysis to be convincing.

Augustine's other answer, therefore, is more decisive, and this is that Rome had help. Roman success served God's purpose. Roman culture was not so unique as to account for her fantastic success and her longevity. Rome was unique and important only because of the coming of Christ. Is it mere coincidence that Roman expansion was essentially complete at Christ's birth and that in the next two centuries Roman power was consolidated during an unprecedented period of relative peace? Christians could never believe that the perfect environment for the transmission of Christianity throughout the ancient world was a mere accident, anymore than they could doubt that Rome's decline indicated that the old empire was no longer an aid but an impediment to spiritual progress.

These things cannot be doubted because spiritual progress itself cannot be doubted. If God is the source of all being, then all that happens must be in accord with His divine plan. Of course, mere mortals cannot grasp this plan, except insofar as God has revealed it directly through His word or He has revealed it indirectly by the course of events. We know that there will be spiritual progress, and we know that there can be no earthly progress. Everything that happens does so for a purpose, but the purpose is never ours. Empires and civilizations will come and go, and earthly history, when seen as a whole, can be nothing but senseless babble. The only history that has any meaning is the history of the faith.

If all that happens is in accord with the divine plan, is God then the author of the senseless political instability and human misfortune that constitutes human history? He is not, for there is one choice He has left to us. We can choose ourselves or Him. If we choose ourselves, we cannot alter the course of things, since that is determined by God's plan. The only consequences that follow from sin are futility, destruction, and pain. If all humans loved God alone, the senseless quest to make ourselves into something other than what He has made us would cease, and so would strife and cruelty. Not God, but our own pride, is the cause of war and political upheaval.

Yet God, omniscient and omnipotent, surely anticipates the decisions we make, and certainly has the power to keep us from sin. From these undeniable propositions stems the doctrine of predestination. They might seem to imply that our decisions are not really free and that God is indeed the author of the evil we do and the misfortune we suffer. Augustine argued that these are false conclusions, confusing God's perspective with our own. Just because God knows how we will choose before we do so does not release us from the responsibility of choice. What difference could it make to us that God knows the future, if we do not? We exist in time; God is the maker not only of us but of time itself. There can be no before and after for God, nor even cause and effect. But these relationships apply to us, and we must accept them.

Moreover, to blame God for our own sin fails to understand the nature of the gift that He has given us. Ultimately, salvation depends on God's grace. Before we can hope for God's grace, however, we must choose God over ourselves. Faith is meaningless without choice, and because of our inherent pride, faith is our only hope. God has given us hope with the burden of choice, and He would not deprive us of this by refusing to let us choose. Our ability to deny God is no limitation of His infinite power, for only He could have given us this choice. And to condemn God for letting us live in a world where we must suffer the consequences of human sin could only mean that one has chosen wrongly.

The Politics of Sin

There can be no worldly ideals for a Christian because there can be no earthly fulfillment. Until we are reunited with God in the hereafter, we are incomplete and, as such, can never attain self-knowledge. Without self-knowledge, notions of self-mastery and personal autonomy are delusions, and without self-sufficiency, visions of freedom and happiness are foolish illusions. Moreover, they are dangerous illusions. Our only hope for salvation is God's grace, and the only hope for God's grace is to struggle against temptation and to beg His forgiveness for our failures.

Given the dangerous futility of worldly ideals, the only aims of a rational politics, other than the maintenance of public order, are to secure an environment free of the grosser sorts of earthly temptations and to facilitate the propagation of the word of God. Those who take responsibility for achieving these aims need to be sober, thoroughly practical people free of idealistic fantasy. Politics is a nasty burden that should be borne by dutiful men and women willing to do what is necessary to preserve the pilgrimage, provide security to the pilgrims, and urge them not to tarry along the way.

A Brief Guide to the Literature

For reasons that should be obvious by now, Augustine is not primarily a political theorist, and there are relatively few full-length studies devoted to his political thought. What may be considered the standard survey of his thought in general is provided by Etienne Gilson, *The Christian Philosophy of Saint Augustine* (1960). Peter Brown's excellent intellectual biography, *Augustine of Hippo* (1967), is not likely to be superseded.

Herbert A. Deane, *The Political and Social Ideas of St. Augustine* (1963), is a highly competent and readable survey of Augustine's political thought. Yet this book is as much a critical assessment as a survey, particularly regarding Augustine's attempt to reconcile the persecution of heretics with his view of the nature of the state. A kinder, gentler Augustine is presented in Peter Dennis Bathory, *Political Theory as Public Confession: The Social and Political Thought of St. Augustine of Hippo* (1981).

In *Whose Justice? Whose Rationality?* (1988), Alasdair MacIntyre considers Augustine as the initiator of one of four important traditions of rational moral inquiry in the West. Yet William E. Connolly's assessment of significance is even more sweeping. In *The Augustinian Imperative: A Reflection on the Politics of Morality* (1993), Connolly argues that Augustine exemplifies the psychological power of the belief in a moral order, as well as the personal costs and political dangers of such a notion.

St. Thomas Aquinas and
the Politics of Salvation

The Historical St. Thomas Aquinas

Except for an episode in his youth, Aquinas's life is not the stuff from
which fascinating biography is fashioned. The seventh son of an aristocratic and moderately influential family, he was born in 1224 (or perhaps
1225) at the family castle midway between Naples and Rome. This is
near the famous Benedictine monastery at Monte Cassino, where Thomas was sent at an early age to be educated. At the age of fourteen,
however, military conflict in the region caused his father to send him to
the University of Naples. This was a mistake. After several years at the
university, Aquinas became a monk, joining the Dominican Order. His
family was distressed. They did not object so much to his chosen voca-
tion as to his choice of the Dominicans instead of the Benedictines. The
Dominicans were a new order, devoted to preaching and scholarship,
with little organizational wealth and relatively low status. His family,
considering his choice both foolish and embarrassing, kidnapped and
imprisoned him in their castle. During his imprisonment they tried various ploys to get him to change his mind. They failed, and after a year he
rejoined his brethren at the university.

The rest of Aquinas's life is unlikely to have much interest to anyone
not intimately involved with interpreting his writings. He continued his
education at Naples, then at the university in Paris, then Cologne, and
finally back to Paris. There he first taught and wrote for publication,
and he did little else for the remainder of his life. Apart from Paris, his
assignments were primarily in his native Italy, and he died near Naples

before reaching the age of fifty. The only remarkable aspect of Aquinas's comparatively short life is what he left behind, his writings. Superficially, the most remarkable thing about these writings is their sheer volume. His most famous and important work, the *Summa of Theology*, is a multi-volume study longer than some encyclopedias. There are many other titles, but it would serve little purpose to list them. Aquinas wrote for theologians, and his works typically were intended to resolve current theological disputes. Modern readers are likely to find them tedious and archaic.

Yet it is not the beauty of prose that compels us to take a political thinker seriously, but the power of ideas. As with Aristotle, Aquinas's political thought is compelling not only because of the force of his arguments, but also because it is part of a comprehensive and coherent philosophical system. There are few topics not discussed or left unexplained. The parallel between these two philosophers is not coincidental. Almost all Aquinas's work is either intentionally or in effect a commentary on Aristotle's philosophical system. Until the beginning of the thirteenth century most of Aristotle's works were unknown in the West, and their sudden availability from the East caused a crisis for the church. It was bad enough that Aristotle was neither Christian nor ancient Jew; even worse, his relatively integrated view of the nature of reality was intellectually superior to any alternative offered in the Christian universities. The first response was to ban the teaching of Aristotle's ideas. The second, more effective response was to interpret these ideas in such a manner as to render them compatible with Christian doctrine. The task was largely undertaken by Dominicans, Aquinas chief among them.

His synthesis of Aristotelian philosophy and Augustinian theology has been enormously influential. Although his works were banned at the University of Paris a few years after his death, less than fifty years later he was canonized. During the Reformation he emerged as the preeminent theologian of Catholicism, a status officially sanctioned by papal authority in the nineteenth century. From his perspective, our sojourn on earth is not nearly so bleak as Augustine would have it, and political authority has a positive, albeit limited role to play in helping us to meet our Maker. His synthesis achieved a worldly philosophy compatible with Christianity. Martin Luther, an Augustinian monk who despised Aristotle, considered such an achievement self-defeating. For Luther, Calvin, and other latter day Augustinians, any effort to reconcile Christian belief with human reason can only serve to undermine the primacy of faith.

Human Nature and Rational Motivation

The separate intellect, according to the writings of our faith, is God Himself, the Creator of the soul, in Whom alone we will find happiness.... The human soul participates in intellectual light coming from Him.

—*Summa of Theology,* I, question 79

For Aquinas, however, faith and reason cannot be in conflict. Whatever the limitations upon our ability to reconcile our belief in God with reason, faith itself requires us to affirm the perfect rationality of God. What is the alternative? An irrational God would be an imperfect God, and an irrational universe would be a universe beyond God's control. No Christian could believe such things. Augustine did not believe them; instead, he held that human reason was so weak that to think us capable of grasping more than a hint of God's plan could only be a symptom of human pride. God's reason is not ours, and the rationality of the universe is of little relevance to us. While not differing greatly with Augustine's assessment of the power of individual reason, Aquinas denied that the weakness of individual reason should lead one to depreciate human reason in general. We are social creatures who depend upon one another, who learn not just from our own experience but also from the experience of others, both living and dead. Although we may never completely comprehend God's plan, at least not while we remain in this world, as a species we are equipped to recognize and appreciate its grandeur.

Yet there is another, more fundamental divergence on the assessment of human nature between these greatest of Christian theologians. As on so many things, they agree that we are sinners, dependent upon God's grace for our salvation. Because, as congenital sinners, we are unworthy of God's grace, Augustine maintained that we could never be certain of salvation, that our only hope was to sincerely beg for mercy. Aquinas in effect assumed the opposite. Salvation is ours as long as we do not foolishly throw it away. Irrespective of whether any of us deserve it, we are already the beneficiaries of God's grace. Did He not send Jesus to save us? Is not the belief that He did so the very definition of a Christian?

God has given us more than hope. He has given us the rational facility to realize our potential for salvation. To identify human nature solely with will, subordinating the role of reason, is in Aquinas's view completely untenable. A will is no more than an inclination, and an inclination cannot exist without an object; it is always an inclination toward something. Consequently, the ultimate object of inclination cannot be a matter of will itself, and free will can only apply to how one acts upon an ultimate or natural inclination. Aquinas accepts Aristotle's characterization of our ultimate end as happiness, and that happiness can be achieved only by fulfilling the inherent, defining potential of our species. As a Christian, he maintains that the ultimate source of human happiness must be God, and that humans have a natural inclination toward God.

And how does one move toward God? Clearly it has nothing to do with proximity in space; the only way mere mortals can approach God is by understanding and participating in His plan insofar as possible. The universe must be rational because it is the creation of a perfectly rational God. Because it is an expression of divine perfection, to understand the rationality inherent in existence is to behold the magnificence of God. Why else would God have bestowed rationality upon us other than to allow us to know Him? Our sojourn on earth is not so much a test of faith as an opportunity to appreciate the beauty of existence and to prepare ourselves for the bliss of complete awareness of God in heaven.

As rational creatures endowed with a natural inclination toward God, we should consider ourselves as junior partners in His divine plan. Obviously, we know very little of this plan, but as Christians we cannot doubt its existence. Consequently, we are obliged to accept the world largely as it is, irrespective of whether we can completely understand it. For the world obviously makes sense in God's perfect understanding. On the other hand, we are also obliged to strive to understand the rationality inherent in existence, as well as to arrange our own human affairs in conformity with this rationality. We are part of God's plan; He did not place us on earth in order to have us reject His creation and pine for the hereafter. We must play our part in God's rational order, and to do so we must use our heads.

To understand, as best we can, and to live in accord with God's rational order is indeed our duty. But such a characterization is misleading, for this "duty" is the basis of human happiness. Aquinas's deity is truly merciful; the faithful and the good will live the most meaningful and happy lives. There is no need to choose between this world and the next. Good Christians need not sacrifice all pleasures of an earthly existence in order to enjoy the incomparable pleasures of paradise. The former, in fact, are simply attenuated versions of the latter. Paradise can only be paradise because of direct experience of God. But the magnificence of God is reflected in His creation, and those who consciously choose to participate in His plan enjoy not just the prospect of salvation but also intimations of His beauty and glory.

The Motivational Basis of Social Solidarity

The custom of the Church has the greatest authority and it is always to be emulated in all matters. Now, since the very teaching of Catholic Doctors receives its authority from the Church, one should rely upon the authority of the Church rather than on the authority of Augustine, Jerome, or any Doctor.

—*Summa of Theology*, II–II, question 10

Like Aristotle, and for many of the same reasons, Aquinas emphasized the social nature of humanity. We are dependent materially, culturally, and intellectually upon our social context. But with Aquinas we are also dependent spiritually. For this reason the most important level of association is not the political community in which one is nurtured, protected, and trained, but rather the civilization that provides the cultural universals and morality without which social and political order would be impossible. The happy life requires a level of social organization transcending principality, city, or nation. The focus of a meaningful life is Christendom, not France, England, the Holy Roman Empire, or even the United States of America.

God's will is unaffected by the ever-changing political jurisdictions characteristic of human association. For God is perfectly rational, and His plan transcends the contingencies of human existence. As a perfectly rational plan, it must be understood as the universal law that governs the world. Human happiness ultimately depends upon understanding and participating in God's plan. Only in this manner can we fulfill our natural inclination toward God and share in the beauty and power of His creation. Obviously, the extent to which we can order our lives in accordance with God's will and find real meaning and happiness is largely dependent upon the degree to which we can understand God's will.

Aquinas calls God's plan the "Eternal Law." Our faith in God requires us to acknowledge the existence of Eternal Law. The fact that we are mere mortals, however, necessarily means that our understanding of the Eternal Law is incomplete; only God can completely comprehend it. Yet we must understand as much of it as is possible for us. The most important reasons for this necessity have already been discussed, and have to do with human salvation and the happiness of becoming nearer to God. In addition to these are the practical considerations of securing a stable and effective social environment. The Eternal Law governs the course of temporal reality; it is not just a set of moral maxims, but rather a universal law promulgated by God. We cannot ignore the natural order of things if we are to have functional families, prosperous societies, and peaceful polities.

Consequently, we must strive to comprehend the Eternal Law and arrange our affairs in accordance with its dictates. How, then, do we acquire this knowledge? Some of it we can gain by our own efforts and some of it is given to us. Aquinas calls the former, that which we achieve by our own efforts, "Natural Law," and the latter, that which is given to us, "Divine Law." Before discussing each in turn, it must be emphasized that both Natural Law and Divine Law are subsumed under Eternal Law, and that they differ only in the manner by which they come to us. Because there is only one God, there can be only one divine plan governing the universe.

Natural Law is possible because we are rational creatures, endowed with the ability to reach general conclusions from experience. Not only can we devise stratagems to cope with the demands of everyday life, we can also discern why these stratagems are effective and necessary. On a moral level, we can see that some patterns of behavior serve no purpose and are ultimately self-destructive. Like Aristotle, Aquinas held that the natural is functional. This assumption follows not just from Aristotle's metaphysics and epistemology, but especially from the confidence that a perfectly rational God would not have created anything superfluous. For the same reason we can be confident that the natural has an inherent rationale that can be grasped and expressed philosophically. Because the natural is rational and, therefore, accessible to all rational creatures, Natural Law is possible for both Christians and heathens. Indeed, Aristotle himself was an unfortunate heathen, yet Aquinas considered him the greatest of all philosophers, almost always referring to him simply as "the Philosopher."

Being a Christian, then, will not necessarily make one a good philosopher, but it does give a decisive advantage in understanding the Eternal

Law. Human rationality is, as Augustine stressed, a frail and unreliable thing, at least by itself. Christians do not need, however, to rely solely upon their own intellectual resources in understanding God's will. They have access to God's word, or the Divine Law. Divine Law is contained in the Bible. Expressed in scripture, it is given by divine revelation. Obviously, revelation requires faith in order to be recognized as a form of knowledge; if a heathen acknowledges scripture as the word of God, then he or she is not a heathen. Because only the Christian has access to Divine Law, a Christian with the intellectual ability to be a good philosopher will certainly be a better philosopher than a similarly equipped pagan.

This is the case because Divine Law and Natural Law are not different kinds of knowledge. As previously indicated, they are differentiated solely by their manner of acquisition. Since we acquire our knowledge of Natural Law through our own reason, we always comprehend its rationality; but since our reason is fallible, we are bound to be in occasional error about what we think is Natural Law. Since we acquire Divine Law through the grace of God, we might not know why it is rational, but we cannot doubt that it is so. Just because it comes from an indubitable Source, we can be certain of its validity and can use it to direct and regulate our own efforts to understand the Eternal Law. Divine Law cannot conflict with Natural Law because they are both expressions of the same Eternal Law. Yet Divine Law is more certain than what we take to be Natural Law. Consequently, Christian philosophers can use the Divine Law as a check on the accuracy of speculative reason, and will make far fewer errors than their heathen counterparts.

But of course they will make mistakes; after all, they are imperfect mortals. Moreover, Divine Law is not given specifically to philosophers, and is frequently expressed in terms appropriate to the particular context and persons to whom it was immediately given. Divine Law and Natural Law cannot conflict, and it must be possible to rationally reconcile all apparent differences. Such a task requires intelligence, diligence, and an uncommon degree of devotion; it is not a job for amateurs. Yet the integration of Divine and Natural Law into an ever-expanding knowledge of God's plan is beyond the intellectual power of any single individual, even of a dedicated Christian sage such as Aquinas himself. All mortals are fallible. Whatever knowledge we do not learn from God we must learn from experience. Yet the experience of one lifetime, one generation, or even one century will not suffice to compensate for our mortal imperfections.

Fortunately, we have the help not only of Divine Law, but also of the experience of many centuries of human speculation. We learn not so much as individuals but as a conscious community of believers, as a civilization devoted to God. Even philosophers are spiritually dependent upon a larger community in their quest to understand God's plan, to discover Natural Law and integrate it with Divine Law. And for philosophers this larger community is not confined solely to Christendom. Knowledge of Natural Law is possible for all rational creatures, and to some extent is known by all civilizations. Indeed, the introduction of the works of Aristotle represented for Aquinas perhaps the greatest single advance in Christendom's knowledge of Natural Law. Yet there is nothing to fear in acknowledging the wisdom of pagans; for God's rational plan is universal, accessible to some degree to all with the power of reason. Given the limitations shared by all mortals, Christian philosophers would be foolish not to make use of the rational achievements of all God's creatures in their effort to understand His plan.

If philosophers are spiritually dependent upon the larger human community, how much more so are those engaged in less lofty pursuits dependent upon Christendom? Although Aquinas, affirming that God's existence could be rationally demonstrated, did not agree with Augustine that a Christian must necessarily live by faith alone, it is certainly the case that most Christians will neither be able to prove the existence of God nor understand the intricacies of the Natural Law. They will have to live primarily by faith in God and trust in the church. Yet they too must share in God's plan. Human institutions must be ordered in conformity to God's plan, and it is important for all Christians to appreciate to the degree possible for them the beauty of His creation. For them, even more than for philosophers, a degree of earthly happiness requires a supportive network of social and cultural institutions. Foremost among these, of course, is the Christian church, led by those devoted to the task of integrating Divine Law and Natural Law, and dedicated to educating all Christians to appreciate the power and glory of God's plan.

The Function and Organization of Authority

Just as men who are associates in a state agree on this point, that they are subjects of one prince by whose laws they are governed, so, too, do all men, to the extent they naturally tend

toward beatitude, have a certain general agreement in relation
to God, as to the highest Prince of all, the Source of beatitude
and the Legislator of the whole of justice.
—*On the Perfection of the Spiritual Life,* chap. 13

There is a fourth type of law, which Aquinas called "Human Law."
This is roughly what we refer to when we speak of law in a legal context. It differs from the other three categories of law in that it is promulgated and enforced by secular authority rather than by God. It also
differs in its content. Natural and Divine Law are not at all different
from Eternal Law; they are just different ways of knowing the Eternal
Law. In principle, their content is the same. Although Human Law must
be compatible with Natural Law, it cannot incorporate all of Natural
Law, and must in some ways extend beyond it. For Human Law must
be practical in the sense that it must respond to the contingencies of
particular social environments. It must take into account public resources, the capacities of subjects, and social customs. Consequently,
Human Law changes. Natural Law may grow, but because it deals with
rational necessities, it never changes.

In recognizing that Human Law has its own imperatives and needs,
Aquinas in effect acknowledges that political authority has a positive
role to play in God's plan. It is not, as it was for Augustine, almost exclu-
sively an instrument of coercion necessitated by sin. Its purpose is never
simply the imposition of order for the sake of stability itself. Just as Natural and Divine Law, Human Law contributes in its own way to earthly
happiness. Indeed, the primary purpose of Human Law is to help people
live in accordance with Natural and Divine Law insofar as they are capable, and this is the primary responsibility of those who formulate and
administer it. This responsibility requires stability, of course, but it is stability for a higher end than simply earthly peace.

Despite the independent content of Human Law and the positive
function of the political authority responsible for its promulgation, theological ends and ecclesiastic authority are ultimately superior for Aquinas. The mere fact that Human Law changes indicates that it is an imperfect law formulated by and for imperfect beings. Because its highest
end is to maximize a population's ability to live in accordance with Natural and Divine Law, Human Law must be guided by the dictates of
these superior, more rational forms of Law. Human Law is inferior because it is a compromise between the rationality of God and the weakness of humanity. Its purpose is to arrange the affairs of a particular

community in conformity to what we know of God's plan insofar as we can do so. But we are not angels in Heaven, and our affairs will inevitably reflect this fact.

Human Law must frequently be accommodated to practices clearly contrary to Natural Law. For instance, usury, the charging of interest, was judged unnatural by Aquinas because he considered it payment for something not consumed, and therefore tantamount to demanding payment for nothing. It is wrong, and in a perfectly rational world such a practice would not exist. Yet he argued that, given present arrangements and levels of mistrust, to prohibit its practice would on balance lead to greater misfortune than its toleration. Moreover, many morally reprehensible and self-destructive practices are simply beyond the power of secular authority to control, both because of its own inefficiency and because popular customs sanction such behavior. Many today consider smoking, gambling, and consumption of alcohol examples of behavior that must be tolerated only because the effort to eradicate them would be futile and counterproductive. Legal authority, Aquinas cautions, should largely confine its enforcement efforts to regulating behavior injurious to others, and often ignore behavior detrimental solely to the perpetrator.

More often than not, however, social custom effectively and beneficially regulates behavior that formal secular authority would be practically powerless to manage. In fact, Aquinas conceptually extends the range of the Human Law beyond the legal sphere to include these customary practices. Most social rules are not technically legal, since they are uncodified and enforced informally through various forms of social censure. Aquinas considers such social regulation Human Law, and social custom actually constitutes the bulk of Human Law. Moreover, he cautions secular rulers against attempting to alter the customary practices of their subjects through legal statutes unless clearly necessary and beneficial. For social order is dependent upon respect for social custom, including to some extent even the inclination to obey the edicts of secular authority.

In addition to its inability to do more than supplement and marginally improve upon social custom, political authority is limited also, and more fundamentally, by the very fact that it has a positive role to play in the quest for human salvation. The exercise of secular authority is a responsibility, not a prerogative. Mere domination does not in itself legitimate authority. Rulers are responsible for maintaining the social and cultural environment encouraging their subjects to live in accordance with God's plan. It is their duty to protect and foster public morality and the institutions through which moral training is conducted. And while rulers may, as a practical matter, be exempt from the coercive power of the Human Law they themselves enforce, they are in conscience obliged to obey their own law. They are responsible for the common good; their rule must be justified by its contribution to the happiness of their subjects, not just their own happiness. Indeed, if unfettered power were the source of their happiness, they would be deficient Christians jeopardizing their own salvation.

Aquinas, like Aristotle, affirms that political power must be constitutional in the sense of being responsible and limited. Unlike Aristotle, however, Aquinas does not dwell on matters of political organization, and he never refers to the "constitution" of a particular regime. In fact, he does not appear to use the concept at all. He does not have to. For while the institutional arrangements of the various political authorities encompassed by Christendom may vary, they must all have the same "constitutional" values. Human Law must be guided by Natural and Divine Law, and this requirement leads to yet another limitation upon the legitimate authority of secular rulers. Although political rulers should be intelligent, devout, and well trained, they must be practical people because their task is to deal with the practical problems of adapting to local circumstances and exigencies. They are unlikely to be highly competent interpreters of Natural and Divine Law. The authoritative interpretation of superior law clearly must be the prerogative of the learned ecclesiastics of the church, those who devote their lives to the integration of Natural and Divine Law.

The church is the only universal institution in Christendom. By Aquinas's logic, political authority should not be universal but parochial. Human Law is an attempt to cope with the practical problems of distinct societies and to accommodate, insofar as feasible, their particular customs and institutions to God's plan. It is the entire community of the faithful, not the parochial political community, that is the focal point of human meaning and commitment. The church administers to this community, and one of the responsibilities of secular rulers is to protect and facilitate the efforts of local clergy in reconciling the vagaries of daily life with the will of God, just as these local church functionaries will give aid and moral support to secular authorities. They all serve the same end, each in their own way. But however deferential the local clergy must be to political authorities, their primary loyalty must be to the more inclusive organization of which they are a part, the church.

In the last analysis, everyone's primary loyalty has to be to the church. If these two levels of earthly institution never strayed from their appropriate functions, there would never be need to choose between them. Yet political rulers, typically and perhaps necessarily being persons of action rather than learning, will occasionally exceed their legitimate jurisdiction. When such injustice results in hardship for subjects, the question of whether they can justifiably disobey their rulers is complex, and will be discussed in the next section of this chapter. When such usurpations concern spiritual matters, however, one must obey God and His earthly representatives rather than any secular authority. Aquinas is never really definitive on the matter, but it would seem that the highest ecclesiastic authority would be obliged to declare any secular power significantly impeding the work of the church an enemy of Christendom, whose authority must not be confirmed by any Christian. If a choice must be made, only a fool would choose local authority over Christendom.

His great esteem for Aristotle should not obscure the radically diminished role of political association in Aquinas's understanding of rational priorities. It is no mistake that he did not discuss constitutional questions of political organization in any detail; they are not all that important. He clearly preferred, all things being equal, an elective monarchy. In his scheme of things this makes sense. The management of Human Law is an administrative, practical task, and a single chief executive enhances efficiency and clarifies responsibility. An elective monarchy increases the likelihood that the monarch will be a capable person chosen for a purpose, rather than a person whose abilities will be determined largely by the accidents of birth and who is likely to view authority as an entitlement rather than a trust.

Moreover, the responsibility of periodically selecting a ruler would require a number of subjects to be involved in the administration of public affairs, and Aquinas believed this to be important for two reasons. The first is practical. Since secular authority aims to supplement and marginally improve upon customary practice, significant involvement of at least the more reputable members of society is probably essential for effective administration. The second reason is more vital. To truly appreciate God's plan, we must to some extent participate in it. For our existence in this world to be happy and fulfilling, we must be His junior partners. Just about the only thing on earth over which we as a species have some significant measure of control is the conduct of our own immediate affairs. We are obliged, not just by convention but by reason, to be responsible family members, reliable neighbors, and dutiful subjects. The more weighty the level of one's public responsibility, the greater one's role in the unfolding of God's plan.

Aquinas's General Theory of Political Change and Stability

Faith in Christ is the origin and cause of justice.... Wherefore faith in Christ does not void the order of justice, but strengthens it. Now the order of justice requires that subjects obey their superiors, else the stability of human affairs would cease.

—*Summa of Theology,* II–II, question 104

Public participation in public affairs is not tantamount to democracy, and Aquinas's endorsement of civic commitment should not be seen as laying the foundations for any kind of popular sovereignty. Except insofar as deep-seated popular sentiments must be accommodated as a practical matter, the will of the people is irrelevant to the conduct of public affairs. Legitimate public order is not a matter of community preference, but of God's will. The ultimate responsibility of secular authorities is to render the human order as commensurate with God's plan as practicality and human knowledge permit. Consequently, rulers cannot consider themselves responsible to those whose behavior they must monitor and hope to improve. Like everyone else, they are responsible to God.

And those excluded from political influence are not necessarily being deprived of anything very important. For political power does not necessarily bring one closer to God. Control over the immediate lives of one's fellow citizens does not ensure effective partnership in the implementation of God's plan. Because it requires constant compromise, the exercise of political power is a difficult and frustrating responsibility. We are not equal in our ability either to discern or to implement God's will. To discern God's will, even to the degree possible for mortals, takes years of study, and requires intelligence, diligence, and devotion. Its effective implementation calls for the same scarce attributes of character, as well as a sense of proportion and a degree of decisiveness. It, too, is no task for amateurs. Involvement in public affairs may increase a person's potential for appreciating the glory of God, but only for one able and willing to accept such responsibility.

Yet it is important that even those best qualified for helping to implement God's plan recognize their limitations. They are mere administrators. The exercise of secular authority does not mean responsibility for providence; we are at best junior partners, facilitators of a grand design that will come to be irrespective of what we do. God is in control of our fate, and it is our duty to help in the realization of His will by fulfilling our rational obligations. Consequently, those who refuse, either from ignorance or depravity, will certainly suffer in the hereafter, and are very likely to come to grief in this life as well. What is true of individuals is even more true of whole societies. Those who would sway the people with impractical and irrelevant ideals of political equality and popular sovereignty, convincing them that it is possible to reorder society in accordance with majority will, only prepare the way for social instability and human misery. To reduce the political influence of the most learned and devout can only serve to undermine rational order, and thereby destroy the institutional and cultural support essential for the salvation of the rest of the population.

The priority of preserving this network of social and cultural institutions, so important for the salvation of common people, cannot be over emphasized. The fear of social upheaval may even require the support of secular rulers who abuse their power, who clearly fail to fulfill their responsibility as rulers. From a strictly individual perspective there is no moral obligation to obey a ruler who has become a tyrant. It is not a sin to resist a tyrant because it is really the tyrant who is guilty of sedition against the commonwealth. Nonetheless, if resistance causes more social upheaval than the tyranny, then the rebellious are as sinful as the tyrant. Given the uncertainties of predicting the consequences of such a drastic measure as rebellion against constituted authority, those who might be willing to risk their lives for the sake of justice would do well to carefully consider the fate of their souls.

To undermine the basis of social and political order is not only sinful; it is stupid. It is stupid irrespective of the ideological goals that might motivate it. The only rational purpose of political authority is to preserve social institutions and perhaps rectify some of their more obvious irrationalities. God's design rules the universe. We can only be facilitators, adapting our institutions as required by the unfolding of His plan. Social existence cannot be reordered through Human Law. Human Law is not a tool; it is an evolving set of adaptations. It must adapt, on the one hand, to changing circumstances, and, on the other, to the slow growth of our understanding of Natural Law. Rational citizens do not enter public life in order to remake the world, but rather to fulfill their rational obligations to play their part in God's order.

They are concerned, in other words, with personal salvation rather than with achieving some sort of political program. Since Human Law is necessarily imperfect, our social arrangements can always be made more rational and just, and it is our duty to take advantage of all obvious opportunities to do so. Yet we must never presume to be able to re-order our society in accordance with a human vision of a perfectly just society. Indeed, we need not be too worried about social progress; because providence rules the world, progress is foreordained. Our primary concern ought to be with the futility of human pretensions and the irrationality of personal ambition. For these are the basic sources of instability in human affairs. If all would attend to their rational obligations and have faith in the wisdom of the Creator, both social stability and personal salvation would be assured.

The Politics of Salvation

Because we are endowed with sufficient sense to appreciate the magnificence of God's creation and to discern our role in His grand design, happiness on earth, if not bliss, is possible. More fundamentally, earthly happiness is possible because we are the recipients of God's grace. The highest priority for any Christian must be to ensure that this gift of grace is not wasted, to ensure the salvation of his or her soul. For this reason, the community of believers is the highest level of human organization. It is Christendom, not Aristotle's polity, that exists for the good life.

Notwithstanding its limitations, the political community, like all human associations serving a rational function, contributes in its own way to human happiness. But citizenship is just one valid social role among many. Parent, spouse, son or daughter, student, teacher, breadwinner, friend, and good neighbor: None of these or numerous other social roles are inherently inferior to citizenship. As rational creatures we need not blindly accept whatever set of social obligations is given by circumstance. Yet most social roles serve a purpose, a purpose we can understand. The dutiful performance of one's rational obligations allows us to live fulfilling lives in accord with God's will. Happiness, therefore, requires that we should be more concerned with our rational duties than our presumptive rights. If citizenship is among our duties, so be it; if it is not, neither our happiness on earth nor our prospects for salvation should be appreciably affected.

A Brief Guide to the Literature

Catholic writers often refer to Aquinas as the "Angelic Doctor." Given the prominence of his work in Catholic theology, as well as his relatively sedate life, it is no wonder that the primary purpose of existing biographies seems to be to explain why he is a saint. An exception is the useful study by James A. Weisheipl, *Friar Thomas D'Aquino: His Life, Thought, and Work* (1974). There are numerous books attempting to briefly introduce the man and summarize his work, although these too are invariably hagiographic. Of these, Martin Grabmann, *Thomas Aquinas: His Personality and Thought* (1963), provides what must be one of the best general introductions to Aquinas's thought. A more demanding, although still accessible overview is given in Frederick Copleston's *Thomas Aquinas* (1955).

Book-length summaries of Aquinas's political thought are relatively rare, and the most prominent among them, Thomas Gilby's, *The Political Thought of Thomas Aquinas* (1958), is highly historical and somewhat lacking in analytical acumen. This is certainly not the case for two shorter discussions of Aquinas's political thought that differ slightly in their assessments of the extent to which Aristotle's influence led Aquinas to diverge from medieval conventions. Alexander Passerin d'Entreves's, in *The Medieval Contribution to Political Thought: Thomas Aquinas, Marsilius of Padua, Richard Hooker* (1939), maintains that Aquinas, perhaps unwittingly, planted the seeds for a fundamental departure. Paul E. Sigmund, in his introductory essay to his anthology of Aquinas's most politically relevant writings, *St. Thomas Aquinas on Politics and Ethics* (1988), tends to accentuate how conventional medieval ideas influenced Aquinas's reading of Aristotle. This is also the thesis of Harry V. Jaffe's meticulous study, *Thomism and Aristotelianism: A Study of the Commentary by Thomas Aquinas on the Nicomachean Ethics* (1952), which may be seen as the critique of an aggrieved Aristotelian.

Given Aquinas's importance as a theologian and the immense differences between his social environment and ours, efforts to adapt or modernize his thought are to be expected. Jacques Maritain's, *Man and the State* (1951), is the most noteworthy attempt to modernize Aquinas's political thought. Maritain maintains that under contemporary conditions Aquinas would be led by the logic of his thought to affirm the secular authority and social pluralism characteristic of Western liberal democracies. Conversely, Alasdair MacIntyre, most directly in *Three Rival Versions of Moral Enquiry: Encyclopedia, Genealogy, Tradition* (1990), offers his Aquinas as an antidote to a moral crisis caused by the supposedly bankrupt philosophical liberalism that we inherited from the Enlightenment.

6

Machiavelli and the
Politics of Glory

The Historical Machiavelli

Like Plato, Niccolò Machiavelli was a citizen of a city-state. He was born in 1469, in the Italian city of Florence, located in the region known as Tuscany. Unlike Plato, Machiavelli took an active part in the public affairs of his city and strongly supported its republican institutions. Indeed, his republicanism and his deep love of politics are the two most conspicuous aspects of both his life and his political thought.

A republic in Renaissance Italy was certainly not a democracy, but rather a regime characterized, on the one hand, by nonhereditary rule and, on the other, by political rights for those fortunate enough to be classified citizens. During Machiavelli's youth, Florence was a republic in name only, being dominated by a powerful family whose wealth and influence derived primarily, or at least originally from banking—the famous Medici. Machiavelli himself was born to a respectable family of very limited financial resources. He was, nonetheless, given the classical education necessary for a career in public affairs. Following the downfall of the Medici and their immediate successors, Machiavelli was given a significant administrative position in the republic.

Rather than a political leader himself, Machiavelli was something of an administrative aide and adviser to some of the political influentials of Florence. As such, he was frequently sent on diplomatic missions and was able to observe politicians in a large number of the Italian states, as well as the courts of the French king and the Holy Roman Emperor.

Italy was a particularly turbulent and dangerous region during the decade of Machiavelli's public service, providing an environment where one could come to appreciate both the subtleties and the brutalities of political and military conflict. Since the Florentine republic was weak and vulnerable, dependent on powerful yet unreliable allies to maintain its independence, Machiavelli's political experience was not only extensive but intense.

In 1512, however, the Florentine republic came to an abrupt end, and with it Machiavelli's political career. The Medici returned to power and immediately purged the government of those with republican loyalties. Machiavelli's hopes of returning to public service were fatally compromised when he was suspected, incorrectly, of participating in a conspiracy to overthrow the Medici. He was arrested, tortured, and imprisoned for a short period. When released, he was banished to his small estate outside the city. Machiavelli never gave up his hopes of returning to a life of public service, and for years attempted to convince the new rulers of Florence that he could be both reliable and useful. Indeed, we are indebted to his efforts to ingratiate himself to the Medici, and to his failure to do so, for the works that have made him famous.

During his involuntary leisure, he wrote, among other less-known works, a classic play (*The Mandrake Root*), a classic history (*The History of Florence*), and a classic treatise on military strategy (*The Art of War*). More germane in the present context are his two classic works of political thought, *The Discourses* and *The Prince*. The latter, a handbook for the politically ambitious offered as a gift to the Medici ruler, has earned its author the reputation of "a teacher of evil" and made his name a synonym for political ruthlessness. Yet his purposes transcended mere opportunism, either his own or those he wished to impress.

Machiavelli's thought was informed by a distinct view of human nature and social reality. Although he wanted a society in which most inhabitants could be moral, such a society could be neither established nor maintained according to a moral code or principles of justice alone. From his perspective, saintliness in politics unavoidably leads to a facsimile of hell. Politicians cannot confine themselves to moral guidelines because politics is inevitably characterized by unintended consequences and irony. Indeed, the final irony for Machiavelli was that just as his efforts to impress the Medici were rewarded with minor public duties, his new patrons were swept from office. He died in 1527, a few months after the new republic had refused him a position because of his carefully nurtured ties with the enemies of Florentine republicanism.

Human Nature and Rational Motivation

If a prince be anxious for glory and the good opinion of the world, he should ... wish to possess a corrupt city, not to ruin it wholly like Caesar, but to reorganize it like Romulus. For certainly the Heavens cannot afford a man a greater opportunity of glory, nor could men desire a better one.

—*The Discourses*, pt. I, chap. 10

Before Machiavelli's conception of human nature can be explored, we must first understand his view of the meaning of history. In a word, history is meaningless. It is meaningless in the sense that there can be neither historical progress nor divine Providence. If there is a God, He will have to implement His own plan by His own inscrutable methods. For those who claim to be His representatives on earth are limited, ignorant, and often self-interested mortals who would only sabotage their own effectiveness if they deluded themselves into believing they understood God's will or had access to divine power.

Divinity being irrelevant to the conduct of human affairs, human beings must rely on their own ingenuity and efforts to achieve their goals. Now if politics could be a matter of applying scientific rules, then we might hope to compensate for our limitations of intellect and weaknesses of will through careful application of method and prudent attention to precedent. Even without Providence, we might hope for progress. But politics cannot be social engineering. Our limitations and weaknesses, as well as our aspirations and willingness to sacrifice, are part and parcel of political reality. These things cannot be predicted on the basis of a set of rules, and for this reason, chance, uncertainty, and frustration are also intrinsic features of social affairs. At best, we can formulate maxims of action in order to enhance the likelihood of achieving our goals, but we cannot consistently foresee circumstances in which such maxims become useless or even self-defeating. Consequently, human endeavor can be successful only temporarily, and there can be "progress" only in the short run.

In the long run there is nothing. Human history is no more than a chronicle of the establishment, growth, decline, and collapse of societies and civilizations, one after another. To paraphrase Shakespeare, a history of humanity could be no more than an aimless story of sound and fury, signifying nothing more than an inexhaustible source of restless energy and ambition.

Mortals, however, are by definition short-run creatures, and the meaninglessness of human history does not necessarily imply that life itself is meaningless. If one could be satisfied solely with some degree of material comfort, one might be able to achieve a satisfactory existence through work, willingness to adapt to changing circumstances, and good luck. Yet such a level of aspiration differs little, if any, from that of cattle, and while it may be descriptive of the lifelong motives typical of most individuals, most people will not acknowledge the fact. Most people must believe they exist for a much higher purpose, irrespective of whether they understand it or whether it encroaches significantly on daily priorities. In brief, most self-conscious creatures of limited aspiration cannot accept the meaninglessness of history and must justify their existence to themselves through faith either in Providence or in progress.

It is perhaps fortunate, then, that limited aspiration and limited curiosity tend to be found together. But what of those with more active minds, who refuse to believe what they cannot understand simply because belief is convenient? Some will refuse to accept the meaninglessness of the universe, becoming theologians or philosophers. A few of these, once they are convinced they have successfully discerned the design or ultimate potential of civilization, may become prophets, disturbing the dormant existence of their less inquisitive fellows by demanding a consistency between ultimate purpose and daily life. This tends to be very unsettling and is perhaps why prophets are usually honored after they are safely dead.

From Machiavelli's perspective, however, it is more rational to be honored by one's contemporaries than posterity. This is not only because of our mortality but more fundamentally because the aspiration for the esteem of one's community, to be a hero, is the only quest both meaningful in itself and compatible with our essentially human capabilities. However one describes these capabilities, they add up to the potential to determine our own fate. Unlike cattle, lions, or foxes, we can do more than simply adapt to a changing environment. Civilization did not spring from the earth like a plant; it was built. Our social and political institutions are not the products of natural growth but the result of willful imposition.

Yet we need only consider our disappointments to realize that we are not in complete control of our fate. Similarly, the ubiquity of political strife gives conclusive evidence that social institutions are almost always the result of a large number of, at best, only partially successful willful impositions. Consequently, it is more precise to say that the distinctive trait of a human being is the inclination to willfully reorder reality, rather than success in the endeavor. For Machiavelli, a meaningful life is a struggle between fate and human will, between *fortuna* and the individual *virtù* required to prevail against adversity. Even individuals of ability fail as often as they succeed. Nonetheless, those having the courage and the ability seriously to attempt to control their social environments, to be effectively political, best fulfill their human potential.

Politics is a highly competitive and risky business, which is why those who engage in it must have courage. This observation inevitably raises the question of the incentives that might justify the risk. Why is it rational for one to risk reputation, domestic tranquility, livelihood, or even life itself in the hope of exercising a degree of control over the course of events? Two mutually reinforcing answers can be found in Machiavelli. The first is simply that comfort and security often require a degree of deference and self-limitation unacceptable to those with great confidence in their abilities. The price of domestic tranquility is usually some form of domestication. Not only does politics offer adventure, it also holds out the prospect of experiencing self-assertion and victory, as opposed to the relatively servile acceptance of the rewards of meritorious service, as determined by received rules and alleged superiors.

The sense of adventure and the experience of one's own capabilities may be sufficient incentives in themselves, but the second reason for the rationality of political engagement is more fundamental. In a meaningless universe the only meaning available is that created by ourselves. For those who cannot justify existence through submission to divine will, the only alternative source of meaning is the esteem of others. Status and reputation, of course, can be gained by conforming to conventional expectations, but this sort of social esteem is not likely to be sufficient for the more capable and independent of human beings. Instead, such individuals will strive to be recognized as leaders, innovators, founders, or even saviors. They will try to be celebrated, rather than merely respectable, and will aim at glory, rather than status. In a word, they need to be heroes, and this is the ultimate ambition of a rational politician.

The Motivational Basis of Social Solidarity

Of all the men who have been eulogized, those deserve it most who have been the authors and founders of religions; next come such as have established republics or kingdoms.
—*The Discourses*, pt. I, chap. 10

Although glory is the most rational stake in political struggle, it is not the most prevalent. The typical motivation in politics, as in most other endeavors, is short-term personal advantage, most frequently of an economic nature. Yet despite any mutual dependence created by pursuit of economic well-being, the primacy of economic concerns is corrosive of the bonds that make communities possible. For social solidarity, in Machiavelli's view, ultimately rests on the individual's readiness to sacrifice, or at least forgo, immediate personal interests in favor of community needs. Consequently, whatever inclines individuals to make such an adjustment in personal priorities provides a basis for social solidarity.

Machiavelli was as much an elitist as Plato, however, and the motivation behind social commitment varies with the capability of the individuals in question. At one point he identified three types of "minds": those that can understand on their own initiative, those that can understand when instructed, and those that simply cannot understand. Although it is not exact, a parallel topology of individual political potential is assumed in all Machiavelli's writings: the ability to make and implement rules, the ability, at best, to act in accordance with existing rules without guidance, and the ability to accept guidance. Those with the first potential we can call "politicians," those with no more than the second, "functionaries," and those limited to the third, "followers." Each type of person is subject to a distinctive motivation toward social commitment.

Politicians, struggling with fortune in order to control their own fate, are compelled to identify that fate with a political community if they are to achieve glory. In our own eyes we may all be heroes, but unless this assessment is confirmed by others, it is likely to be hollow. If glory is what ultimately gives meaning to politics, then politicians can be seen as attempting to build living monuments to themselves. Indeed, some political leaders actually have created the communities that worship them as founders decades after their deaths. Although these may be extreme cases, political heroes are invariably revered because of supposed contributions to the protection or improvement of their societies. The extent, therefore, that the politically ambitious seek fame is the extent to which they must commit themselves to the creation or protection of some sort of social constituency.

Instead of glory, which is reserved for great feats or innovations, the social commitment of functionaries rests primarily on the desire for social honor. Honor supposedly is given in recognition of faithful, meritorious service, and it can take many forms. These include public awards, titles, positions of responsibility, and privileges of rank. All this comes down to social status, but social status of a publicly sanctioned kind. If status is imparted by birth or purchased with wealth, an individual is more likely to feel that society is in his or her debt than vice versa. Status is likely to lead to social commitment only when it is publicly bestowed in recognition of services rendered.

These services can require diligence, competence, and perhaps courage above and beyond the call of duty, but they cannot require political risk. Functionaries, let it be remembered, can be effective within an existing set of expectations or accepted standards, but they do not have the ability to make their own rules or establish their own standards. This is why the desire for social honor and status ties them to the community. It is not gratitude for the recognition that leads to social solidarity, but dependence on society as the source of honors. Medals and titles issued by a defunct political entity are as worthless as its currency.

Socially committed followers are important to both politicians and functionaries, since they provide the adulation that makes heroes and the deference that defines social status. Not only this, they also provide the cannon fodder often required for glory and the taxes or labor absolutely essential for the maintenance of the majesty of the state and its capacity to bestow honor. They provide all this, yet they receive so little in return. Social honor or rank is forever foreclosed to the masses, and whatever glory they experience is vicarious at best. So why do the followers follow?

A number of answers can be provided, all depending on the limited skepticism natural to those who need guidance. Of the benefits of government, for instance, security is perhaps the most fundamental as well as the most obvious. Yet governments engage in offensive as well as defensive wars, and even in the latter they typically fail to yield to clearly superior forces until much needless suffering has occurred. Whatever the real or supposed benefits offered to the populace by governments or political leaders, there are times when the cost becomes manifestly exorbitant to even the most unsophisticated of citizens. Consequently, governments and leaders cannot rely completely or primarily on practical benefits in order to gain unquestioned support from followers. Indeed, unquestioned support is usually most needed when the ability of authority to provide benefits is low, when followers simply must be asked to sacrifice.

Instead of benefits, therefore, governments and leaders must depend on *myths*. A myth, as the term is used by Machiavelli, is a religious or ideological justification of authority. The truth of a myth, by Machiavelli's analysis, is irrelevant to its effectiveness. Truly effective myths, however, not only must give reasons for obeying authority but more fundamentally they must rationalize codes of moral conduct. For although governments cannot guarantee physical security with any great consistency, authority typically maintains its legitimacy by claiming to secure another dimension of the social environment, the moral order. Indeed, the security of the accepted moral order, if it exists and is perceived to be threatened, is of greater priority to common people than physical security. This is because certitude in a moral order thwarts a greater threat than injury or even death. This threat is the sense of meaninglessness, which undermines the willingness to try to overcome the obstacles to life as opposed to the ability to do so. With neither glory nor social honor, and without the capacity to act independently, the masses must affirm the existence of a meaningful order and support on faith those who claim to preserve it.

The Function and Organization of Authority

Good examples are the result of good education, and good education is due to good laws; and good laws in their turn spring from those very agitations that have been so inconsiderately condemned by many.

—*The Discourses*, pt. I, chap. 4

Just as social institutions are the largely haphazard result of will and effort, so too is their preservation. Inertia counts for little in human affairs except decay and decline. Consequently, however distinctive the tasks taken on by any particular government, the most fundamental must be the preservation of the conditions of its own existence. And however unique the circumstances and diverse the response to them, there are two general conditions for the maintenance of governmental authority. The first is to ensure that the population remains willing to support and obey authority, and the second is to meet the challenges of a constantly changing environment. These two tasks may seem obvious, but in fact they require incompatible patterns of behavior.

The sources of social solidarity, of course, are likely to be the most important sources of obedience and support. As discussed in preceding paragraphs, the masses' support of a regime can be expected as long as they believe it to reflect the certitudes justifying moral order and self-respect. Consequently, in order to ensure the support or acquiescence of the greater part of the citizenry, it is very important for the government to propagate and protect the conventional creed by which most individuals judge the worth of one another and themselves. The exact nature of this creed and the myths by which it is rationalized vary with the culture and history of each particular society. Although Machiavelli believed popular creeds invariably include traditional or religious elements, in our time nationalism would seem to have compensated in part for the diminution of these dimensions of conventional morality.

Not only is a legitimating myth necessary to ensure the acquiescence of the general population, it is also crucial in securing the support of those I have called functionaries. As previously discussed, this stratum of the population will sacrifice immediate personal interests in favor of those of the community primarily for the personal distinction of publicly certified status. Since functionaries are limited to the pursuit of honor, as opposed to glory, they require relatively unambiguous criteria of how to go about earning it. In other words, not being able to establish their own standards, they require conventional definitions of what is honorable, of what will automatically give them the respect and deference they seek.

If these conventional standards are to result in social deference, they must be in harmony with popular moral certitudes. Both the manner by which honor is attained and the emblems by which status is paraded, therefore, must be compatible with whatever myth rationalizes the prevailing moral creed. Consequently, it behooves a government not only to justify the standards it uses to award special recognition to those who serve it in terms of the legitimating myth but also to ensure that these standards are not too blatantly compromised by personal favoritism or financial graft.

If support and obedience were the only conditions of effective authority, then there would be no need to accommodate the aspirations of those I have called politicians. For one thing, their number is always very small. More important, their existence is a constant threat to the sanctity of the myths on which governments depend for support and obedience from both the people and the functionaries. This is because those who are confident in their ability to make their own rules cannot be relied on to observe conventional standards when it is inconvenient or costly to do so.

Yet politicians are essential to the effective functioning, and even the survival, of government. For no matter how firm the popular belief in a myth, or how compatible the distribution of honor with conventional standards, governments must periodically act in ways incongruent with their legitimating myths and the principles derived from them. This is because a given set of rules cannot provide adequate guidelines for unanticipated events. Given the uncertainty intrinsic to social affairs, unprecedented situations are not rare, and reliance on established procedures is frequently counterproductive. Individuals who depend on received wisdom are not likely to possess sufficient creativity to cope with the unprecedented.

Indeed, in the long run those most sincerely committed to the prevailing myth are least capable of maintaining its plausibility. For while faithful adherence to a moral code enhances its credibility in the short run, moral flexibility is essential for its survival. As unforeseen predicaments require innovative practices and policies, it is necessary to give new interpretations to the myth if it is to be adapted to new circumstances. Inevitably, reinterpretations will occasionally contradict past practices and doctrines, and these too must be modified or ignored. Such flexibility is very difficult for the faithful. Politicians, in contrast, are likely to maintain a relatively pragmatic orientation toward legitimating myths. That is, they will not be prevented by scruple from doing what necessity demands. Dangerous as the unscrupulous may be, they have a decisive advantage in adapting to an ever-changing environment.

One of the requirements for a rational organization of political authority, then, is to give politicians the responsibility for making new rules as circumstances dictate. Another, just as important, is to give these same politicians an incentive to protect conventional standards and constitutional principles they do not, indeed cannot, accept as a personal code. In addition, a rationally organized government must employ and give public honor to its functionaries on the basis of merit, measured by services rendered to the community and its leaders. Finally, an optimally constructed political system would reinforce popular commitment to its legitimating myth, identifying itself with the conventionally accepted moral order. Only a republic has any hope of meeting these requirements.

As indicated at the beginning of this chapter, a republic is not, for

Machiavelli, necessarily a democracy. Instead, it is a regime in which rulers are held legally responsible for their conduct and can be replaced if they lose the confidence of the community. This is not tantamount to democracy because the institutions that supposedly monitor the performance of leaders might be dominated by the wealthy or some other form of elite. Yet however restricted political influence, in a republic some legal rights are enjoyed by all residents who hold citizenship.

So defined, republics allow the fulfillment of all four requirements for a rational organization of political authority. First, the fact of citizenship encourages the populace to identify with the political community. Second, the absence of a hereditary ruling aristocracy enhances the likelihood that positions of influence and status will be awarded primarily on the basis of service and merit. And if leaders must retain the confidence of the community to gain and remain in office, those who lead are more likely to be those willing to risk reputation in a competitive struggle for preeminence and glory. In short, they are more likely to be politicians. Moreover, those who succeed in the struggle for power have every incentive to preserve the myths that sustain the political faith of the masses and the loyalty of the functionaries. For the loyalty of the latter is essential for governing and the faith of the former is a condition for glory. Glory is precluded for unsung heroes, and only those who consider themselves a people will sing the praises of its founders and protectors.

Machiavelli's General Theory of Political Change and Stability

There are two methods of fighting, the one by law, the other by force: the first method is that of men, the second of beasts; but as the first method is often insufficient, one must have recourse to the second.

—*The Prince*, chap. 18

Yet even the best-organized republic will inevitably degenerate toward futility and chaos. All social institutions eventually suffer the same fate. There are two reasons for this inevitability. The first follows from the meaninglessness of history. Not even the most capable politician will always be able to adapt to the unpredictable. Whether natural catastrophe or the emergence of powerful competitors, external threats beyond the control of leaders are unavoidable, and eventually fortune overwhelms the best defenses.

The effects of the other reason for decline, while just as inescapable, might be postponed through policy and political skill. This is because its sources are internal to a society, rather than external. Social solidarity requires a legitimating myth, but as a society achieves military security and material wealth the myth becomes less relevant and, therefore, less effective. In short, the more successful a political society, the greater the corruption of its population. The more attention they devote to luxury and comfort, the less citizens will be susceptible to claims of civic duty. Without adversity, especially in the form of common danger, individuals become egotistical and unwilling to sacrifice for the sake of the community. Functionaries become unreliable, and the common citizens become cynical, incapable of hero worship. Society becomes divided into self-interested factions or classes, impotent in the face of any external threat that might accelerate its descent into chaos.

Decline is inevitable in the long run. But we are short-run creatures, and there are a number of short-run factors leading to instability that we might hope to stifle. Most of these factors concern the existence and effectiveness of institutions enhancing the prospects of real politicians and simultaneously holding them accountable. For Machiavelli, accountability does not mean control but the replacing of leaders incapable of coping with external threats, unable to maintain the confidence of the populace, or unwilling to tolerate the existence of opposition. Given the previous discussion, it should be obvious why leaders must be able to cope with external threats and maintain popular confidence if stability is to be achieved. But the importance of political opposition might not be as apparent, and yet it is crucially important for understanding Machiavelli's republicanism, as well as its limits.

Legitimate opposition is socially functional because it encourages alternative policy proposals and provides incentive for political ambition. These effects increase both the stock of useful knowledge and the pool of capable leaders available to a political system. Of course, opposition means political strife, and one might presume that this is likely to have repercussions for political stability. To the contrary, Machiavelli holds that political struggle is actually a stabilizing factor, for as long as opponents can fight by legal means, they will have less reason to resort to violence. Moreover, if capable individuals have no hope of attaining positions of power by legal means, there will always be a ready pool of leaders to incite and take advantage of every opportunity for insurrection. For this reason, aristocracy breeds revolution by excluding genuine politicians from the lower strata, and simultaneously producing pretentious mediocrities unfit to rule and unwilling to follow.

Yet open competition for power among the politically ambitious has its dangers as well. Nobody really likes to be held accountable, especially to those one considers inferior, and nobody wants to be displaced by rivals. Intimidation or violence is an ever-present option, and an ever-present threat, for the practical politician. It is also a threat to the political community. For if leaders resort to physical coercion too frequently, fear and distrust undermine the potential for effective collective action. Frequent use also increases the likelihood that violence will be used ineffectively, which is an even greater danger to stability. For retaliation in kind is the almost inevitable result, initiating a process leading to civil war if left unchecked.

Politics is a form of struggle, and the threat of violence can never be eliminated. It can be checked, however, by creating conditions that make it a costly option to use. Although Machiavelli's institutional suggestions are sketchy and equivocal, he recommends some sort of division of power, especially between popular and elite factions. This ensures that all major factions are not so desperate as to resort to extreme means and that they have organization and leadership to defend themselves if need be. Such institutional safeguards, albeit essential, are insufficient by themselves to inhibit politicians. In the last analysis they must restrain themselves. Given their propensity to take conventional morality lightly, only the logic of their ambition can be relied on to reinforce institutional restraints. Glory is reserved for those who establish or protect, not to those who only destroy or simply prevail. In a viable republic an overt use of violence is likely to be seen as an act of destruction.

There will be, even in well-established republics, politicians who will take the risk. Indeed, some will have no qualms in destroying republican institutions in order to enhance their own power. Individuals frequently select domination and notoriety over fame and glory. And since we are all short-run creatures, they may never regret their shortsightedness. Machiavelli considered such individuals evil. But if their unscrupulous opportunism is not to give them a competitive advantage, those who compete with them must also be free of scruples. This is yet another reason why politicians cannot fully subscribe to moral conventions. The important point here, however, is that the means employed can be limited only by the ends they serve, and republics depend on the victory of those who seek glory over those who simply wish to rule.

Since decline and corruption are inevitable, there are inevitably periods of political chaos when these questions of republican stability are largely irrelevant. No political community then exists to appreciate its heroes, and political power ultimately rests on wealth and military might. Those seeking glory in such conditions might be well advised to pursue art, science, or philosophy, rather than politics. To be sure, great glory could be earned by laying the foundations for a republic, but the prospects for success would deter all but the foolhardy. In such circumstances, active politicians will be adventurers in a dangerous game of survival, more warlords than statesmen. To paraphrase Machiavelli, politicians will have to fight like animals rather than human beings, combining the violent courage of the lion with the deceptive cunning of the fox. Life for these adventurers is likely to be exciting, but neither inspiring nor glorious. Few of them will prosper or even last very long, especially if they become preoccupied with convincing their contemporaries that they are heroes.

Nevertheless, republics emerge from such conditions because the practical imperatives of survival force even these political thugs to lay foundations for viable political communities. In this highly competitive environment, those who can more effectively draw on combined resources and act in concert with others have the competitive advantage. In general, politicians either can attempt to forge alliances with the powerful or they can attempt to mobilize popular support. They cannot do both because the powerful, irrespective of whether they consider themselves an aristocracy or simply an oligarchy, are primarily concerned with dominating the people, while the people are primarily concerned with escaping the exploitative domination of the powerful. By Machiavelli's analysis, the astute politician, when there is a choice in the matter, will try to build support with the people, rather than the notables.

Not only is it easier to win popular support, it is also more reliable once it is won. It is easier because the populace typically wants only to be free of capricious interference in its daily affairs and to be protected, while notables want distinctions and privileges. It is more reliable because the populace, especially in a very unstable environment, will view a leader as a protector, rather than a servant who can be dismissed when convenient. Furthermore, encouraging a populace to consider itself a people or a community is crucially important militarily, in that it makes possible citizen soldiers ready to sacrifice their lives for their families and country. Indeed, according to Machiavelli, the only effective way to prepare for an adverse shift of fortune, to bank as it were one's *virtù* as a politician, is to cultivate the support of a people.

Apart from providing security, the most effective ways to cultivate popular support are to foster collective myths and to grant legal rights. Paradoxically, politicians indifferent to personal glory, the foremost short-term threat to republics, are pushed by the practical imperatives of political struggle to establish a political context in which the pursuit of glory is feasible for those few endowed for it. For the rest, the pursuit of social honor or at least a certain civic virtue becomes possible, and avarice and indolence revert to the mundane meaninglessness of daily life, where they belong. In a republic, one can hope to be all that one can be. Although in the long run republics may be no more stable than other kinds of regimes, their inherent advantages in the management of conflict and the creation of collective purpose ensure that they will periodically emerge from the vicissitudes of anarchy.

The Politics of Glory

Since glory and fame do not exist in the absence of an appreciative population, Machiavelli's elite, unlike Plato's, is radically dependent on the community. Political leadership is not undertaken out of a sense of duty but is something for which one struggles. Ambition inevitably results in competition, and a successful regime will be one in which contenders for power are able to compete politically, rather than militarily. In such a regime rival politicians have a chance to earn the popular acclaim they seek by protecting and strengthening the community. And when they fail, there will always be able contenders to take their place.

Although popular rule is impossible, an open, competitive political system requires a significant degree of popular politics, where power rests on community support. Of course this support is typically gained as much by the manipulation of communal myths as by substantive achievements. But most of us really want no more from authority than security and the reinforcement of the conventional illusions on which our sense of moral worth rests. We do not want to rule. We want our rulers to be accountable, but we do not want to be responsible for what they do. We are not gamblers. Let them have the glory, but let them take the risks. If they succeed, let us honor them. If they fail, let them expect nothing better than contempt.

A Brief Guide to the Literature

Through the centuries, Machiavelli's very name has become a synonym for expediency and ruthlessness. As a result, interpretation almost inevitably involves a degree of apology or condemnation and typically focuses on the question of Machiavelli's intentions. Consequently, it is important to have some knowledge of Machiavelli's life and environment before exploring the secondary literature. Felix Gilbert, *Machiavelli and Guicciardini: Politics and History in Sixteenth-Century Florence* (1964), and J.R. Hale, *Machiavelli and Renaissance Italy* (1960), are both highly readable and reliable accounts of the political and intellectual context in which Machiavelli worked.

Sydney Anglo, in *Machiavelli: A Dissection* (1969), argues the unique thesis that Machiavelli was not a systematic thinker and that all those who find unifying intent behind his diverse writings both misinterpret and overrate the man. J.G.A. Pocock, by contrast, in *The Machiavellian Moment: Florentine Political Thought and the Atlantic Republican Tradition* (1975), attempts to demonstrate not only that Machiavelli was a thinker of uncommon power and scope but also that he contributed in a major way to a republican consciousness eventually culminating in the American revolution. Leo Strauss also believes Machiavelli's work to express theoretical unity and thinks its influence on Western political thought to have been immense. But Strauss, in *Thoughts on Machiavelli* (1958), maintains that this influence has been unfortunate, that Machiavelli intended to undermine the political influence of religion and traditional ideas of natural law.

Mark Hulliung's *Citizen Machiavelli* (1983) also paints a relatively diabolical picture of its subject, and in large part is intended to counter interpretations such as Pocock's. In contrast, Sebastian de Grazia's Pulitzer prize-winning biography, *Machiavelli in Hell* (1989), presents a much more attractive image, contradicting that drawn by either Strauss or Hulliung. Yet the whole question of Machiavelli's intent is secondary from a social scientific perspective; what is primary is the extent his thought provides useful conceptual categories for understanding contemporary political phenomena. From this perspective, the thesis of Harvey C. Mansfield, Jr.'s *Taming the Prince: The Ambivalence of Executive Power* (1989) is noteworthy. According to Mansfield, Machiavelli is the inventor of the notion of executive power, and this concept has foreclosed a more viable sense of governing rooted in Aristotle's thought.

Similarly, Hanna Fenichel Pitkin, in *Fortune Is a Woman: Gender and Politics in the Thought of Niccolò Machiavelli* (1984), explores the contemporary implications of an ambiguity in Machiavelli's thought.

7

Hobbes and the
Politics of Fear

The Historical Hobbes

Born prematurely in an English coastal town threatened by the Spanish Armada (1588), Thomas Hobbes wrote that he and fear were born twins. He lived through a dangerous period of civil strife, and for the most part he depended for his livelihood on the favor of those wealthier and more powerful than himself. His political thought is based on fear of an ultimate evil, rather than aspiration toward an ultimate good. Yet Hobbes was a contentious, independent fellow who did not hesitate to involve himself in controversy and, occasionally, place himself in danger because of his beliefs.

Hobbes was raised by an artisan uncle. He had been abandoned at an early age by a father of modest means who was forced to flee after an assault on another man. Despite his unauspicious origin, Hobbes was able to take advantage of educational opportunities to distinguish himself as a student and promising scholar. After receiving a degree from an Oxford college, he had the good fortune to be employed as a tutor to the heir of a wealthy and powerful family. For thirty years, with only slight interruption, Hobbes had access to a fine library, traveled to the cultural capitals of Europe, and enjoyed the company of the most learned individuals of his day. During this time, he translated a number of classical works into English, including a famous translation of Thucydides's history of the Peloponnesian Wars.

Encountering geometry for the first time when over forty years of age, Hobbes adopted its method of reasoning and wrote the first of his political works, the *Elements of Law*. This early defense of the monarchist position aroused some antagonism, and Hobbes found it prudent to move to Paris, where he managed to live for eleven years. Before long he was joined by the remnants of the monarchist party after their defeat in the Civil War and the eventual beheading of Charles I. Hobbes was employed as a tutor in mathematics to the heir of the lost throne, despite distrust over his reliability and religious views by some in the exiled English court. These fears were magnified after the publication of Hobbes's greatest work of political thought, the *Leviathan*. Instead of arguing for the divine right of kings, Hobbes argued that despotic power was necessary to achieve social peace, that monarchy was an essential expedient, rather than something divinely sanctioned. Any dictatorship, irrespective of its claims to royalty, would seem to qualify.

Perhaps confirming such suspicions, Hobbes now found it prudent to return to England and accommodate himself to the rule of Oliver Cromwell, a decidedly nonroyal dictator. With the restoration of the monarchy, his former pupil, now Charles II, not only protected him from retaliation from ecclesiastical and court enemies, but even granted him a pension. He devoted the remainder of his life to scholarship and science, engaging in numerous controversies with some of the greatest pioneers of modern science. He died in 1679, at the age of ninety, no doubt professing to the end his timorous nature and love of peace.

Human Nature and Rational Motivation

What is the *heart* but a *spring,* and the *nerves* but so many *strings,* and the *joints* but so many *wheels* giving motion to the whole body such as was intended by the Artificer?
—*Leviathan,* pt. I, Intro.

As discussed in the corresponding section of the chapter devoted to Plato, rationality conceived as no more than calculation cannot provide an adequate basis for a conception of human nature. Yet more than any of the great political thinkers, Hobbes characterized humans as calculating machines. Nonetheless, while illustrating the significant extent to which our thoughts and emotions are mechanical in their operation, he really presents a powerful argument for the social and personal futility of unconditional self-interested calculation. For in the final analysis, his view of social and political rationality rests on a very nonmechanical moral maxim. Whether Hobbes himself was completely aware of this need not concern us. As dictated by the social scientific perspective adopted here in the reconstructing of his thought, conceptual coherence is a more important goal than fidelity to an author's intention.

This perspective is particularly appropriate in the case of Hobbes, in that he himself was attempting to lay the basis for a science of society. His view of science, however, is not based on careful observation of natural regularities, nor even on the experimental method. Instead, Hobbes adhered to a view of science strongly influenced by the thought of the great philosopher René Descartes and the example of the great scientist Galileo. While the truth of theories can be illustrated or demonstrated by observed effects, valid scientific theories originate in a skeptical application of deductive reasoning. Only deductive logic can give us certain truths, but skepticism is required because deductive logic leads to correct propositions only if it proceeds from clearly self-evident axioms. All the suppositions of received opinion or the doctrines of learned scholars must be considered as no more than groundless speculation unless rigorously derived from the elementary, self-evident facts of experience.

For Hobbes, the most basic of these self-evident facts is provided by the Galilean view of physical reality, namely, that the universe is nothing more than uniform matter in constant motion. The variety of the objects encountered in experience and their diverse characteristics result from the multitude of combinations by which this moving matter may interact with itself. Irrespective of this variety, however, all things are composed of the same "stuff."

Consistent perhaps to a fault, Hobbes was prepared to apply this perspective in understanding human nature.

We, too, are matter in motion, although, as we later see, our self-consciousness dictates that we are a little bit more than this. But like all other animals, we are primarily complex machines motivated by hedonistic gratifications and aversions. The difference between the higher and lower forms of life is that the latter react to the external environment in an instinctual manner, while the former can learn by experience, by projecting past experiences into the immediate future. The difference between human beings and other higher forms of animals is that humans can do more than simply project past experiences; we can reduce past experiences to elements that we imaginatively can reconstruct into future possibilities. From these mentally constructed scenarios we can choose which course of action might best maximize our desires and minimize our aversions. In a word, we can think.

Yet thinking is no more than calculation and therefore requires no more than the complex, essentially mechanical circuitry of an incredibly powerful computer. We need not presume a "soul" or some sort of nonmaterial vitality. We are simply a machine stimulated by a constant stream of externally generated sense impressions. Nonetheless, thinking does depend on an ability unique to humans, which is language. Our ability to speak is essential to thinking because we cannot reduce experiences down to components that we can reconstruct into future possibilities unless we can assign an identifying *name* to each component. To calculate efficiently we must be able to reason logically from the elements of experience. As it is in science, so too in everyday thinking.

Unfortunately, the source of our advantages over other animals, language, is also the source of our greatest weakness, our propensity to delude ourselves. Other animals may make mistakes, but they cannot tell lies either to themselves or others. Since they cannot classify, they can be neither inconsistent in classification nor fix illusionary things in their minds by attaching a name to them. We, in contrast, have a propensity to distort reality by combining a number of simple, unconnected experiences into complex, fantastic images. We alone among the animals often see only what we want to see, or sometimes want things that do not even exist. Under the pressure of our emotions, we are liable to be intoxicated with our own imaginations.

The purpose of Hobbes's political science is to minimize the effects of self-delusion in political affairs by deducing rational guides for social aspiration from the self-evident components of human nature. One of these components is the ability to think or calculate, which is supposedly unique to humanity. Another we share with the rest of the animal kingdom, which concerns the goals or motivation behind all thinking. As previously indicated, all animals are motivated by a hedonistic attraction to the things in our external environment that gratify and are repelled by things that cause pain.

Unless perverted by illusion, the various emotions are simply the registers of the frustration and elation experienced in the pursuit of gratification and the avoidance of pain. Things to which we are attracted we feel are *good*, whereas things to which we have an aversion we feel are *evil*. A desire combined with the belief in the likelihood of satisfaction is *hope*; a desire without such a belief is *despair*. An aversion combined with the expectation of harm from the object is *fear*; the same thing combined with the hope of avoiding the harm is *courage*, and a rush of courage is *anger*. Constant hope is *confidence*, and constant despair is *timidity*. And so it goes, all the emotions reduced to some combination of desire and aversion, conditioned by perception and estimate of prospects.

With both humans and many other animals, the emotions can lead to self-defeating behavior if they are so strong that they interfere with perception and undermine the prudent comparison of the present with past experience. With humans, they often undermine the careful application of method and consequently lead to irrational behavior. The most dangerous of the emotions is unique to humanity, however, and this is *vainglory*. Glory itself is, according to Hobbes, simply the elation that comes with contemplation of one's own ability to attain felicity and is really the same emotion as confidence. But when derived from flattery or the result of mere imagination, rather than based on a calculated estimate of real power, it can only lead to vain action and is therefore called vainglory, or vanity. Yet futility is not the real danger of vanity. Instead, it is the madness of self-love in which vanity usually results. Vanity leads to pride and the delusion that the sources of gratification are internal, rather than external. As we see in the following discussion, when the human machine looks at itself as something other than a machine, it malfunctions.

Since the real objects of motivation are provided by the external environment, rather than fixed inclinations or innate principles, there is no "ultimate good" to which we all aspire, by which we can impartially judge ourselves and one another. In fact, an ultimate good that is the final end of our activity would be fatal to life, which is no more than a peculiar form of matter in motion. We must remain in motion to live, attempting to move from one gratification to the next. Instead of a distinct ultimate good, our highest aspiration can only be the condition of "felicity," the continual satisfaction of a string of desires. We could never know, or even really want, a condition of "bliss" in which we were free from all desire. Being incompatible with the fundamental components of our nature, this condition must be one of those imaginary goals we are prone to invent for ourselves.

Despite the lack of an ultimate good, there is an ultimate evil, which is death. The fear of death in animals is probably instinctual, as it might be to some extent in humans as well. But as thinking creatures we are aware of our mortality and our vulnerability. This aversion to death cannot be attributed to an avoidance of pain, since death need not be painful and can in some circumstances be seen as the cessation of pain. Moreover, from Hobbes's perspective, mere mortality cannot in itself be a source of rational anxiety. For the aspiration for immortality, whether literally or figuratively through fame, could be attributed only to the delusion of vanity. Despite his brilliant description of humans as calculating machines, Hobbes does not derive the primacy of the fear of death from a hedonistic calculus. Death is simply an abomination for a self-conscious creature, and the basis of at least a minimal morality.

The Motivational Basis of Social Solidarity

To this war of every man against every man, this also is consequent: that nothing can be unjust. The notions of right and wrong, justice and injustice, have there no place. Where there is no common power, there is no law, no injustice. Force and fraud are in war the two cardinal virtues. Justice and injustice are none of the faculties neither of the body nor mind.... They are qualities that relate to men in society, not in solitude.

—*Leviathan*, pt. I, chap. 13

Fear of death, the ultimate evil, is the key to Hobbes's social and political thought. It explains why rational individuals will want to form a political authority and why they will obey it. In other words, Hobbes derives his principles of rational legitimacy from the fear of death. His argument could be compelling, however, only if the threat of premature death is something that must always, in all circumstances, be taken seriously by any rational person. This is exactly what Hobbes argues. Death is an ever-present threat because the conditions for mutual destruction are entailed in human nature. Only a stable political authority can keep us from killing one another.

There is nothing in Hobbes's conception of human nature that justifies any assumption that we are particularly aggressive animals. His argument is not based on aggressive instincts, or even on a particularly pessimistic view of the human inclination toward peace. It is simply that if left to our own devices, we will soon find ourselves in a *situation* in which we will be forced to defend ourselves aggressively, all the while wishing for peace and security. Rational people are motivated not so much by the desire to conquer and assert themselves as by insecurity and fear.

To develop and elucidate the implications of this argument, Hobbes relies on a device called the *state of nature*. He is, in fact, the first of three great political thinkers to use this device, Locke and Rousseau being the other two. They are called "social contract theorists" because they envision rational individuals creating a government by agreeing to a contract among themselves. Of course, the terms of the contract that rational individuals would insist on are the rational principles of political legitimacy. Which terms are rational depends on the purposes the government is supposed to serve, and these in turn depend on why a government is needed by rational individuals. It is the purpose of the state-of-nature device to discern these purposes. A social contract theorist envisions a situation in which there is a complete absence of political authority in order to isolate the necessary and essential functions of government for rational humans.

Such a state of nature, for Hobbes, is a state of equality, since any special endowments of strength or intelligence can give only a fleeting advantage to any individual. In the absence of some institutional means of binding individuals to consistent relationships, the strong will eventually be outsmarted, the smart overpowered, and even those who are both strong and smart have to sleep. Moreover, the presence of an obvious threat will cause prospective victims to unite temporarily. No one would have a long-term advantage over anyone else, at least one that could be counted on. For the most part, then, each of us is free to pursue felicity as well as circumstance allows.

In fact, however, nobody is going to enjoy a significant degree of success in this lifelong quest. For despite the impossibility of establishing stable patterns of domination in the absence of institutions of authority, everyone is going to be forced to try to dominate his or her neighbors. All are engaged in a quest to gain the objects that bring gratification and to avoid those that bring pain. Inevitably, there is both competition and, more important, insecurity in any state of nature. Others want what you want, and they also are likely to want what you have if you have anything. In a competitive environment lacking stable relationships, extreme insecurity must prevail because all behavior is unpredictable; everyone must be seen as a potential aggressor. When everyone is a potential aggressor, and everyone is more or less equal, the prudent strategy is the preemptive strike.

Consequently, the pure state of nature is a war of all against all. Humans do not especially want to dominate one another; they simply want to enjoy life and avoid pain. But in a state of nature this requires that they secure an extremely uncertain environment, and the only way they can do this is by seeking power over their neighbors, as their neighbors will over them. It is not aggression that fuels this anarchic struggle, but fear. Nor is it irrationality that leads to aggression; on the contrary, aggression results from a valid assessment of what the situation demands. The unpleasant result of rational, calculated behavior in an environment lacking political authority is a war of all against all where, in Hobbes's words, life is "solitary, poor, nasty, brutish, and short."

In this situation, one will cease to be concerned with gratification and pain and instead will be concerned with survival alone, and by any means necessary.

Given this situation, we should expect that rational individuals would attempt to make agreements among themselves to put an end to it. But without authority to enforce agreements, they are only as good as the trust that individuals can have in one another. Insecurity destroys trust, and there can be none in a state of nature. To illustrate, consider the plot of scores of gangster films. The participants are in a state of nature because they have decided to profit from illicit enterprises such as gambling, prostitution, and smuggling. They are motivated by the luxury and status that hugh profits can buy. Yet they unavoidably compete with one another for lucrative markets. Not being able to avail themselves of the courts to resolve disputes or protect markets, they engage in military conflict. Finding military conflict not only very bad for business but also extremely dangerous, the statesmen of the underworld work out a deal to divide markets or territories and settle disputes through some sort of collective consultation. All are reassured and go about their business, until one of them fears that another may be planning to take advantage of decreased vigilance to encroach forcibly on his or her territory, presenting the others with a fait accompli. Knowing that the suspected party will simply deny the suspicion, whether true or false, the fearful one attempts to strike first. It is the only rational option, and it initiates yet another round of gangland terror.

Some might say that it could not happen to a nicer bunch of people, but Hobbes's point is that without authority there is no distinction between legal and illicit endeavors, and we all would be forced to act in a similar fashion. Moreover, we should not assume that gangsters enjoy war any more than we would. All rational individuals fear death and will do what they must to avoid it. All will hope for peace, and this hope is what drives rational individuals to political society. Only through the creation of a power capable of enforcing agreements can we escape the lethal logic of the state of nature. Just as the gangsters of movie lore, however much our terminology may differ, we too need a Godfather.

Just as the fear of death leads to conflict in the state of nature, so too does it compel us to submit to a higher authority.

The Function and Organization of Authority

A multitude ... are made *one* person when they are by one man or one person represented, so that it be done with the consent of every one of that multitude in particular. For it is the *unity* of the representer, not the *unity* of the represented, that makes the person *one*. And it is the representer that bears the person, and but one person; and *unity* cannot otherwise be understood in multitude.

—*Leviathan*, pt. I, chap. 16

Rational individuals will desire to reach agreements with other individuals in order to minimize discord and insecurity. What is needed in the state of nature is assurance that agreements will be enforced, since in this uncertain situation there can be no basis of trust to support them. Indeed, in the state of nature anyone trusting another to act contrary to self-interest is a fool. The solution is a basic, self-enforcing agreement that serves as the guarantee of all other agreements into which individuals freely enter. This is the social contract; by establishing a political authority, it creates the conditions for its own enforcement.

The terms of the contract are very simple. Its purpose is to create an enforcer. Consequently, each individual promises to obey a sovereign authority and observe its laws. The promise is practically unconditional. The sole exception would be occasioned by a sovereign threatening an individual with death. Since the purpose of government is to preclude a situation in which death is a constant threat, a rational individual would not bind him- or herself to submitting when the sovereign threatens death.

On the surface, this may appear to be a rather one-sided agreement. Actually, only the result is one-sided: All power is lodged in the sovereign. But the sovereign does not agree to anything; he or she remains in the state of nature. The agreement is only among the citizens. The sovereign is simply a beneficiary of their agreement. We may picture the state of nature as a group of distrustful individuals all armed with swords, suspiciously eyeing one another. As they circle around, each watchful of the proximity of any of the others, they would all agree that they are in a terrifying circumstance, with none trusting anyone's promise of nonbelligerency. The solution is that they arbitrarily choose one of their number as their leader and agree to drop their swords at his or her feet, to pick them up only at his or her command. He or she will be both their protector and their master. With their allegiance at his or her disposal, anyone not agreeing to obey will be destroyed, which includes those who might renege on their commitment to the others to do so.

What do the subjects get from their voluntary obligation? First and foremost, they escape the constant threat of death. The sovereign has no reason to kill his or her subjects, for insofar as they live up to the agreement making them subjects, they represent no threat. Indeed, they are a resource to the sovereign. It is the fear of death that would have led the first person in the simplistic scenario of the previous paragraph to take the risky decision to throw down his or her sword. Given the potential consequences, calculation alone would not have led one to do it. But we would take the risk because any act offering a realistic hope of overcoming the threat of death is morally obligatory. Whatever hardships the sovereign may impose on the subjects, they will be nothing compared to the evil of death. The second benefit is the ability to pursue felicity by their own efforts and through binding agreements with one another. Although the sovereign's laws will constrain this quest, they simultaneously create the secure, predictable environment where it may find at least partial fulfillment. All in all, the civil state is a great improvement over the state of nature.

The answer to the question of what the sovereign gets from the arrangement is more problematic. Of course, the sovereign will enjoy greatly enhanced powers to achieve felicity. But we should not conclude that a sovereign will enjoy life, nor even live a long one. For the sovereign remains in a state of nature, which is a state of insecurity and rational fear of the most terrifying kind. A sovereign must constantly contend with other sovereigns, and can never trust them. Without a worldwide sovereign to enforce them, treaties and other agreements in the international realm are only as good as the momentary interests of the parties concerned. Prudent nations can never neglect their defenses. The only significant difference between a pure state of nature and international relations is that sovereigns are not necessarily in a state of practical equality.

Two important consequences for the organization of political authority follow from the sovereign's continuing residence in a state of nature. The first is that the sovereign power in the long run must be exercised by a single individual. Hobbes did not, apparently, draw this conclusion, but if logic requires that the sovereign remain in a state of nature, it also requires that he or she remain alone. For no one in a state of nature can count on anyone else also in a state of nature. They must eventually consider themselves enemies. If the social contract, therefore, is to end the constant threat of war, only one person in a given society must exercise sovereign power. The sovereign may have advisers and ministers, but he or she cannot have equals if authority is to serve its purpose.

The second consequence of the sovereign's continuing residence in the state of nature is that the sovereign is not subject to his or her own laws. The laws of the sovereign apply only to the subjects, for they are the only ones who have obligated themselves to obey them. Because the sovereign is not a party to the basic compact creating a political society, the sovereign is not responsible to his or her subjects. Any attempt to hold the sovereign responsible to a basic, constitutional law is in reality a violation of the subject's obligation to other subjects to create a sovereign power capable of enforcing all subsequent contracts that subjects make with one another. For if the sovereign is denied the freedom of choice that everyone has who is in a state of nature, then everyone will be in a state of nature when constitutional disputes occur. No one then will possess the authority to resolve a constitutional issue. When such issues are considered of vital importance, the insecurity each must feel eventually will lead to civil war. The sovereign must be a dictator, preferably benign, but above all strong and secure within his or her own realm.

Hobbes's General Theory of Political Change and Stability

If this superstitious fear of spirits were taken away, and with it prognostics from dreams, false prophesies, and many other things depending thereon by which crafty, ambitious persons abuse the simple people, men would be much more fitted than they are for civil obedience.

—*Leviathan*, pt. I, chap. 2

While the state of nature is a constant threat, avoided only by the presence of a sovereign power, it is a logical construction rather than a description of a particular state of affairs. In the absence of a sovereign, *rational* individuals will be led to act as if a state of nature existed, and the longer they are without a sovereign, the closer will their environment approximate such a condition. The fear of such a state will cause rational individuals to support whatever effective power exists, irrespective of whether it was originally established by election, fraud, conquest, or accident.

Logical constructions based on the calculations of rational individuals are rarely descriptive of reality, however, and Hobbes was not so naive as to believe that mere contemplation would be sufficient to maintain social stability. Clearly, the sovereign would be well advised to demonstrate his or her power occasionally. For although a rational sovereign would not wish to undermine the wealth and capabilities of his or her subjects, since these are resources that can be used in the struggle with other sovereigns, a healthy fear on the part of subjects of the power of authority and respect for their sovereign's willingness to impose his or her will are probably essential.

Yet, by itself, power, like reason, is insufficient. Subjects must be given positive incentives to meet their mutual obligations to the sovereign. For the masses, religion and myth supply these incentives, and it is essential that the sovereign's authority extends to the religious and educational institutions administering to the irrational fears of those intellectually unable to appreciate the rational threat of the state of nature. Indeed, the contribution of Hobbes's own work to the maintenance of social stability is largely confined to demonstrating their proper function to those charged with educating the populace and explaining the nature of things. Professional experts and the official or self-appointed defenders of religious ritual have an understandable tendency to presume that knowledge or revelation provides an independent, nonarbitrary source of authority. Hobbes's work was intended in large part to call into question this self-serving and socially dangerous presumption.

Yet other, less intellectual elites could not be expected to act consistently in conformity with long-term, rational interests without more tangible incentives. The sovereign cannot be everywhere, and those whom he or she relies on to administer the realm have ample opportunity to increase their chances of felicity by occasionally exempting themselves from the sovereign's law. The fear of death is hard to remember when the prospect seems remote. For taken individually, such transgressions do not undermine the sovereign's authority, especially if they are covert. When they become frequent and flagrant, however, the sovereign's strength is sapped and contention among his or her ministers will inevitably increase according to the logic of the state of nature.

To combat this logic, the intelligent sovereign must once again create positive incentives, although myth and religion will not do the trick for these privileged elites. Instead, they must be provided with honors, and their privileges must be firmly bound to these honors. A person's *honor,* in Hobbes's view of things, is simply the value that others attribute to one. Personal value, or worth, is simply one's price, or how much "would be given for the use of his power."

We honor those to whom we wish to ingratiate ourselves, and we feel especially honored when others seek our help or obey us, since both actions at least tacitly acknowledge our superior power. We are concerned with our reputations because a high assessment of our worth gives us a competitive advantage in the continual quest for felicity. It does so, however, only in a civil state.

There is no honor in the state of nature, where all are equally worthless because none has the power to escape misery. Just as the sovereign makes possible trust, so too honor. Just as sovereign power is the basis of all effective law, so too is it the ultimate foundation of personal dignity and social respect. To maintain itself, the sovereign power must insofar as practically possible monopolize the distribution of individual honor and social status. Political and economic elites invariably are highly sensitive to social status and individual distinction, however ignorant they may be of the political precondition for the very existence of these things. Consequently, if the sovereign is seen as the primary source of social honors, the violation of the laws will be seen as a foolish risk of reputation. Moreover, the unmasking of law breakers will itself be a profitable and lawful method to rid oneself of rivals and enhance one's own social honor.

So there we have it, religion for the masses, honor for social and political influentials, and knowledge for intellectual elites. The sources of instability are, for the most part, simply the converse of these sources of stability. The most frequent threat to the power of the sovereign and the public peace comes from social and political influentials, whose constant concern for personal honor renders them particularly susceptible to that uniquely human form of madness, vainglory. They presume that their honor is not value that others put on them but stems from some inherent, individual virtue. This presumption easily leads to another, that authority is obliged to recognize and cater to these supposed individual virtues. Even more than the ambition it often rationalizes, this sense of inherent individual superiority is the fount of sedition.

While the vainglory of the influential may be the most frequent source of instability, it is not the most dangerous. Far worse are the potential repercussions of the presumptions of the intellectuals, especially preachers. For the masses never rebel unless led by those who appeal either to their immediate and obvious self-interest or to their anxiety for salvation. The former makes them collaborators in sedition, the latter the cannon fodder of revolution. Revolution is a faster and much surer path to the state of nature than sedition, and elites who would mobilize the masses against constituted authority on the basis of a principle represent the greatest threat to public peace and personal felicity. It follows that those who find their principles revealed in great or holy books, or given by some method other than deductive reasoning from basic facts, are more dangerous than ambitious, self-interested schemers. An Aaron Burr or Benito Mussolini is much to be preferred over a Thomas Jefferson or an Adolf Hitler.

From a Hobbesian perspective, this point requires continual reiteration because the choice of a sovereign cannot be a solitary or even a rare event. Because there can be no higher, constitutional law limiting the sovereign will, there can be no logically compelling rules governing succession. Logically, the subjects are thrown into a state of nature every time their sovereign dies. Of course, logic does not rule the world, and there usually are conventions in any stable society that allow for peaceful transfers of power most of the time. Logical persons will do well to observe these conventions as long as they suspect that most of their fellow subjects, either through blind habit or prudence, will do likewise. Nevertheless, conventions do not always hold sway. When they cannot be counted on and a choice of a potential master must be made, the rational person will, all things being equal, go with the self-interested realist, rather than with any who promise salvation or justice.

The Politics of Fear

For the rational citizen, public order is not simply the highest of all political priorities; it is the only political priority. All other political goals are the business of the sovereign and become the concern of citizens only to the extent that the sovereign enlists their aid in pursuing public ends. Politics should not be seen as a form of collective decision making or as a public trust and certainly not as a means of aspiring toward moral ideals. Politics is ultimately the nasty business of survival for a sovereign who remains in a state of nature.

Citizens are responsible only for performing legally prescribed duties, which for most will mean nothing more than obeying the law and paying their taxes. Those employed as "public servants" serve the sovereign who employs them, rather than their fellow citizens. Moreover, they serve because of the benefits of employment, rather than from a sense of duty to some common good. As mere instruments of the sovereign, their responsibility is confined solely to giving effect to the sovereign will. Naturally they serve at the sovereign's discretion, since the only political right is the right to live.

A Brief Guide to the Literature

As of yet, Hobbes's life has not received the benefit of an extensive biography, although Arnold A. Rogow's relatively brief account, *Thomas Hobbes: Radical in the Service of Reaction* (1986), is useful. A sophisticated overview of the man and his thought is provided by Richard Peters's *Hobbes* (1967). Many studies explore one aspect or another of Hobbes's influence on, and his reception by, his contemporaries. One of the most fascinating is Steven Shapin and Simon Schaffer, *Leviathan and the Air Pump: Hobbes, Boyle, and the Experimental Life* (1985). In this case study of a scientific dispute, Shapin and Schaffer highlight the difference between Hobbes's understanding of science and that of such empiricists as John Locke or J.S. Mill.

A number of interpreters, however, have depreciated the relevance of Hobbes's approach to science for an understanding of his political thought. Howard Warrender, in *The Political Philosophy of Hobbes: His Theory of Obligation* (1957), argues that it is impossible to derive principles of moral obligation from scientific theory. If Hobbes's principles are valid, they must be morally obligatory on the individual irrespective of the existence of a sovereign power, however necessary such power might be for their social realization. Similarly, although from a much different perspective, Leo Strauss, in *The Political Philosophy of Hobbes: Its Basis and Its Genesis* (1952), contends that Hobbes must have a nonscientific basis for human obligation just because his view of the universe is so empty of anything distinctively human. Strauss forcefully argues that the fear of death anchors Hobbes's political thought and that this premise derives its moral status from a view of human nature predating his commitment to scientific thinking.

Among those who believe Hobbes's commitment to science to be an essential aspect of his political thought, two relatively distinct lines of argument have emerged. The first focuses on the character of scientific reasoning, rather than its substantive results, and is well represented by Michael Oakeshott, *Hobbes on Civil Association* (1975). From Oakeshott's perspective, the unifying thread of Hobbes's thought is his rationalism, the insistence that all true understanding depends on reducing things to their elemental components and establishing through deduction the necessary connections among these components. The second line of argument is best represented by Thomas A. Spragens, Jr., *The Politics of Motion: The World of Thomas Hobbes* (1973). According to Spragens, Hobbes's view of the natural world served as a paradigm for his analysis of the nature and potential of the political world.

A recent work by David Johnston, *The Rhetoric of Leviathan: Thomas Hobbes and the Politics of Cultural Transformation* (1986), provides support for those who affirm the importance of Hobbes's commitment to scientific thinking for understanding his political theory. Johnston maintains that much of the language of *Leviathan* that is seemingly difficult to reconcile with his materialistic psychology is intended to undermine the inclination of his contemporaries to think in nonscientific terms, to reduce their resistance to logical analysis. By this account, Hobbes's primary intent in writing *Leviathan* was not so much to expound his ideas with maximum clarity but to change his readers' mode of thought. In other words, the book had a rhetorical, rather than an expository, purpose. Since political theorists, at least from a social scientific perspective, do not share such an intent, such language might best be discounted in making sense of Hobbes if Johnston's analysis is correct.

8

Locke and the
Politics of Rights

The Historical Locke

John Locke's political thought is significant because it is the classic statement of Liberal democracy. Liberal democracy is representative democracy, based on political equality, majority rule, and respect for individual rights. As a matter of historical fact, however, Locke championed neither political equality nor democracy in his own day, and it is an open question whether he saw such implications in his most important essay on political thought. Some commentators even question his commitment to universal individual rights, pointing to presumed inconsistencies between his political thought, written to influence his immediate contemporaries, and his more considered philosophical work. Indeed, some argue that the similarities between Locke and Hobbes are great and the differences are relatively minor.

We have no need of another Hobbes, but it must be granted that there are striking parallels in the early lives of these two English philosophers. They were near contemporaries; Locke was born in 1632, forty-four years after Hobbes, and died in 1704, only twenty-five years after his predecessor. Both were born in provincial towns to families of modest means. Through the patronage of local notables, both were able to attend Oxford University, and both hated the classical curriculum and scholastic teaching style. Both eventually came to espouse scientific thinking as superior to the authority of the classics. But here the parallels end. For Locke turned to medicine, rather than mathematics, and his science was experimental, rather than deductive.

Despite his disdain for the conduct of education at Oxford, he accepted a teaching position and remained for fifteen years. He was rescued from academic obscurity through the chance acquaintance of a powerful political figure, Lord Ashley, soon to be Earl of Shaftesbury. Locke joined Shaftesbury's household as a physician and soon had saved the earl's life by supervising a dramatically unusual and dangerous operation. No longer a mere physician, Locke became a close political confidant and personal friend, serving Shaftesbury off and on for over a decade, until the earl's death in 1683.

This collaboration turned into a hazardous enterprise, for Shaftesbury became the leader of the parliamentary forces opposed to the constitutional claims and religious policies of Charles II. Both of Locke's famous political tracts, *A Letter Concerning Toleration* and *The Second Treatise of Government,* were written in support of his patron's activities. *The Second Treatise,* it seems, was intended to justify a plot to prevent the succession of Charles's brother to the Crown. All this was patently illegal, and in due course first Shaftesbury and then Locke were forced to choose between exile or possible execution.

Shaftesbury died in exile, but Locke prospered, at least intellectually. In the five years he stayed in Holland, he completed his famous work of empirical epistemology, *An Essay Concerning Human Understanding.* In 1689, Locke was able to return to England in the wake of the "Glorious Revolution," when William and Mary deposed James II, the brother of Charles II. In the same year Locke published all three of the books previously mentioned. The *Essay* made him an intellectual celebrity, and the two political works, although he never acknowledged their authorship, confirmed his status as a champion of English liberty and the new regime. In the last years of his life he was a figure of both intellectual and political influence.

Whatever the similarities between Locke and Hobbes, the respective purposes of their political writings were diametrically opposed. Hobbes tried to rationalize absolute royal authority, Locke tried to rationalize limits on royal authority. Critics of Liberal democracy maintain that the only way he could do so was to give ultimate power to a majority, either of all citizens or of wealthy property owners. In either event, they argue, he did not rationalize limits on this power or provide any real justification for individual rights. From a social scientific perspective, however, there is little to be said for a modified and somewhat less coherent Hobbes. Consequently, the task of this chapter is to present a consistent and persuasive Liberal democratic Locke, a champion of individual rights and limited government. Our purpose is not to dismiss the Liberal individualism associated with his work but to be able to see it as a potentially viable conceptual option based on a distinct view of human nature.

Human Nature and Rational Motivation

God gave the world to men in common; but since he gave it to them for their benefit ..., it cannot be supposed he meant it should always remain common and uncultivated. He gave it to the use of the industrious and rational—and labor was to be his title to it—not to the fancy or covetousness of the quarrelsome and contentious.

—*The Second Treatise of Government*, chap. 5

Locke's conception of human nature is more complex but less developed than that of Hobbes. It is implicit in Locke's rendition of the "state of nature," which, like Hobbes, he constructs in order to discern the rational incentives and legitimating principles of political authority. Yet Locke's state of nature is a far different place than Hobbes's because its natives are far different. Instead of being ruled by anarchy and terror, humans pursue their individual interests with respect for one another's rights and even cooperate with one another when their interests overlap. In other words, the state of nature, a state without political authority, would not necessarily be a state of war. Instead, it would be governed by the rules of reason that constitute the laws of nature.

Locke, of course, assumes that the inhabitants of this state of nature are rational, just as he assumes an environment of abundant resources and the absence of external threats. These assumptions are theoretically necessary. To discern the *rational* principles of legitimacy, extraneous considerations of practical necessity unique to particular circumstances must be removed from consideration. This is the purpose of the state-of-nature construct. There is another assumption, however, clearly entailed in the picture Locke presents of the state of nature: not only must its inhabitants be rational, but there must be a rational and knowable law of nature.

Yet Locke means something far different than Aristotle when he refers to natural law, for he does not believe that nature is guided by natural purpose or final causation. Like Hobbes, Locke denied the existence of an objective moral order to which we are naturally inclined to conform. All ideas, including moral principles, originate in experience;

there are no innate ideas present at birth, waiting to blossom as we mature. An individual's mind, to use the Latin phrase associated with Locke's argument, is originally a *tabula rasa,* a blank slate. Simple ideas become fixed in our minds as the result of observation, or sense perception, guided by our wants and our past experience of satisfaction. A child's notion of food depends on what is given when he or she is hungry, just as his or her initial notion of parent is largely the recognition of the provider of food and warmth. More complex ideas are created by compounding the simple ideas formed by sense impression, a process of association determined by the faculty of imagination as well as by experience of regularity and conjunction.

When Locke refers to natural law, he is not referring to anything written in the hearts and minds of all humans, for initially nothing is written there. Instead, he is referring to conclusions that all rational individuals would acknowledge as valid. Thus, natural law is not innate in either us or the universe, but only represents rationally compelling conclusions derived from experience. Hobbes essentially agreed with this definition, but believed rules had to be deduced from self-evident axioms (such as the fear of death) to be compelling. For him, the universe was simply matter in motion. The application of skeptical reasoning allows us to detect certain principles determining some natural interactions, but the universe itself is a chaotic place, ultimately irreducible to the logical models we construct to understand it.

For Locke, in contrast, the universe displays a high degree of regularity. As demonstrated by the scientific accomplishments of his famous friends Isaac Newton and Robert Boyle, experimental method and careful observation disclose that reality is governed by laws that express its uniformity. Since the universe conforms to these elemental laws, individuals experience the same uniform reality. Prudent, rational individuals, therefore, will naturally come to a consensus on matters pertaining to immediate experience. Humans will inevitably disagree over complex philosophical, religious, or scientific ideas, those compounded from simple ideas. But common-sense notions derived from daily interactions with oneself and one's environment are homogeneous and predictable. Common sense is common because it is based on relatively simple ideas, close to immediate experience.

Consequently, in a hypothetical state of nature rational individuals would not only realize the futility of mutual warfare, they also would be confident that others know this as well. Almost everyone knows it, even in existing societies. Obviously, what most would be doing in the state of nature is attempting to provide for themselves and their families, since this is clearly a natural necessity and what all species do. The distinctive characteristic of humanity is the manner in which individuals provide for themselves. In short, all animals work, but only humans produce. Other species labor to consume the natural fruit of the earth, either as gatherers or as predators, but only human beings increase what is naturally given through agriculture and manufacturing.

Through productive endeavor, we learn to cultivate fields, to domesticate animals, and to fabricate commodities and tools. Production provides both the experiences and the incentives for the development of the arts and sciences collectively known as civilization. Yet more fundamentally, production provides purpose and meaning to life. For productivity is a form of creation. To speak in the Christian idiom common to Locke and his readers, God created the earth and its inhabitants, and to those He created in His own image He gave a divine spark; they, too, could share in the creation of the earth. This, perhaps, is their compensation for having to labor like other species. The important point, which does not require Christian faith to appreciate, is that it is indeed compensation; through productivity we have the opportunity to experience a sense of both individual accomplishment and individual creativity.

We are not gods, however, and we must use what we create to survive and make our earthly existence tolerable. We need, therefore, a means to appropriate and distribute wealth. Moreover, being mere mortals, we need evidence of our accomplishment and creativity as a basis for self-esteem, our assessment of our worth as human beings. Both needs are satisfied by the institution of private property. Locke insists that private property would exist in a state of nature because all rational individuals are capable of acknowledging what belongs to them and what belongs to others. Private property is a natural right, based on reason, rather than legal convention.

Property does not depend on deeds or titles of ownership. Instead, it is created by human labor. In a state of nature, were I to cultivate a field or construct a piece of furniture, I have mixed my labor with the natural fruit of the earth and thereby have made it an extension of myself. It is mine, and were you to come across my vacant abode, you would know that its contents belonged to another just because you are a rational person. If you had so little respect for yourself as to take my belongings rather than work for your own, you would know that you were stealing and would act accordingly, surreptitiously, fearful of being apprehended.

This is no way to live, and most rational individuals would choose to obey common sense and respect one another's property. Not only would they avoid fear and insecurity, they would preserve the conditions of self-respect. For even in a primitive state of nature, in which individuals must work hard to make their way, one can have pride in accomplishment. One's expanding estate testifies to his or her worth as a human being. Consequently, one could live a meaningful life in a state of nature. Rational producers could and would cooperate when interests coincide, and when interests conflict they could resolve tensions through common sense and mutual accommodation. It clearly is in their interests to do so.

The Motivational Basis of Social Solidarity

It is not every compact that puts an end to the state of nature between men, but only this one of agreeing together mutually to . . . make one body politic. . . . For truth and keeping of faith belongs to men as men, and not as members of society.
—*The Second Treatise of Government*, chap. 2

Nonetheless, there would be disadvantages to the state of nature compelling rational individuals to leave it. One of these is obvious; it is the likelihood that a number of individuals will be thieves or worse. According to Locke, such degenerates would be constrained by a form of vigilante justice in a state of nature. It is simply common sense that rational individuals would help one another apprehend and punish violators in order to secure the environment for all. Clearly, however, it would be a great inconvenience to do so, and a formal authority to enforce the laws of reason would be beneficial. Similarly, collective action could more effectively accomplish a number of tasks advantageous to all rational producers. For example, land transportation in a state of nature would undoubtedly be confined to a haphazard network of poorly marked trails. Without a system of roads, the productive advantages of trade and regional specialization would be limited to coastal areas.

Much more important in this regard is a standardized monetary system. Some form of money would develop spontaneously in a state of nature, such as wampum among some of the natives of North America or gold and silver bullion among most of the people of Eurasia. The original incentive for a medium of exchange is to circumvent yet another natural law of common sense, a law that potentially imposes a limit on human productivity. This is the law of spoilage. In brief, it is irrational to accumulate more than one can use, especially if the resource accumulated becomes unusable to anyone else. Since money is good for nothing except exchange, it can be accumulated without limit, unleashing individual productivity, resulting in a higher standard of living for all. Money must be standardized through coinage, however, if a significant level of economic development is to occur. Without mints, there will be no banks.

These are certainly sufficient reasons to wish for a common authority, but such benefits would not by themselves lead rational individuals to create such a dangerous entity as a government. For what greater predator exists than government? What damage could a madman such as Hitler do without a state? The best protector of life and property must also be seen as their greatest threat. None of the conveniences of government could justify its risk.

Rather than the lure of convenience, brute necessity would compel rational individuals to leave a state of nature. For it is not the irrationally shortsighted criminal who constitutes the greatest threat to life and property in a state of nature, but ourselves. Nobody can be relied on to be fair when judging his or her own case. We cannot count on our own rationality when our property is at stake in a dispute. Property is quite literally an extension of ourselves, intimately bound with our sense of self-esteem and personal success. We can be no more objective about our estates than we can about our children.

As in Hobbes, fear provides the most fundamental motive for social solidarity. But it is not fear of one another so much as fear of ourselves and our limited rationality. We need a common, rational judge. The state of nature by definition lacks such a judge. Disputes inevitably occur, even among neighbors of good faith. The more they cooperate in the pursuit of shared interests, the greater the likelihood of divergent interpretations of mutual obligations. To the extent individuals can be rational, these disputes could be resolved amicably. Yet without a common judge, conflict among self-interested producers always threatens to terminate mutually beneficial cooperation and may even result in violence and insecurity. All the things that rational people can do together, and know they should do, such as cooperation in the control of degenerate criminals, are liable to become difficult if not impossible.

This is not a Hobbesian state of war, and these are not Hobbesian people. Their plight is not caused by the logic of the situation but by an inherent defect in their character. It is a commonly acknowledged defect. Sober, rational people often (but not always) compensate for it in daily life by refusing to participate in decisions when their impartiality might be questioned. Just as it is possible to compensate for the defect in personal life, so too is it possible to compensate for it socially. In a state of nature we would need a common judge, and as rational creatures human beings have the ability to create such an authority well before violent conflict becomes an endemic feature of their social environment.

The Function and Organization of Authority

The great and chief end ... of men's ... putting themselves under government is the preservation of their property.... For though the law of nature be plain and intelligible to all rational creatures, yet men, being biased by their interest ... are not apt to allow of it as law binding ... to their particular cases.... There wants a known and indifferent judge with authority.

—*The Second Treatise of Government*, chap. 9

Government is an unfortunate necessity. Its primary purpose is to protect life and property, and its secondary propose is to facilitate productive endeavor. Although necessary, it is no more than a tool. As such, it is legitimate only when used appropriately for its appropriate purpose. It follows that only those who know what is or is not appropriate have any business using the tool, especially since it is subject to misuse. At first glance, these considerations might seem to justify a severe restriction of political rights. Yet this would follow only if political expertise required extensive study and great skill, and such is not the case for Locke. The purpose and proper use of government are as plain as the purpose and proper use of a nail hammer.

Like any tool, government is a human creation. It is created in order to help implement a natural law we can know but cannot always follow. Only natural law gives us claims over one another, and we cannot transfer to a political authority any more right than we would have had in a state of nature. Natural law is no more than rational consensus. Rational consensus in turn results from common experience of a uniform reality. By its very nature, natural law is self-evident; it does not require a high level of intellectual achievement. This is not to belittle the importance of abstract, complex ideas, but only to emphasize that it is foolish to expect consensus on such ideas, whatever their importance or usefulness. Given the tentative nature of their conclusions, neither theology nor science can justify collective authority, and expertise cannot justify political privilege.

Who, then, is to exercise political authority? Since all rational individuals can be expected to understand the purpose of government, only the irrational, such as children, the mentally retarded, and criminals, can be excluded from sharing political power. Consequently, authority must be exercised by a collective, legislative body in which all rational citizens have the right to participate or be represented. As a practical matter, of course, collective bodies almost always resort to majority rule in making decisions. It is, therefore, a majority of rational citizens that ultimately should exercise political authority.

But there is a more basic rationale for the principle of majority rule. Government is necessitated by our need for a common judge to decide private disputes. Since we cannot be counted on to be rational when our property is in question, we need a rational third party. Yet how are we to ensure that the third party will be rational? Any individual or relatively small company of individuals will be subject to the same limitation requiring government in the first place. The purposes of government, then, will not be served if either one person or a small proportion of subjects monopolizes power. He, she, or they cannot be counted on to be impartial, to judge in his, her, or their own case. The best assurance of a rational third party is a majority of rational individuals, for if one cannot trust a majority of fellow citizens to be rational, one cannot trust any human agency.

Clearly, the legislative authority must be exercised by a legislature composed of rational citizens. The executive power, which could be the responsibility of a single individual, must be limited to enforcing legislation approved by a majority of the legislature. In other words, the executive has no legislative authority. Whatever discretion an executive exercises in responding to emergencies and unforeseen circumstances, he or she must be ultimately responsible for such decisions to the legislature. The legislature itself must be open to all rational citizens, both because this is a condition of rationality, or impartiality, and because rational citizens would consent to obey an authority only if their particular interests were represented in some fashion. An impartial third party is a benefit only given the assurance that one's case will be considered.

What, then, will a representative legislature following the principle of majority rule do? More specifically, does majority rule in this context mean that a majority will do as it pleases without regard to the rights of those who find themselves in the minority? From Locke's perspective this is not a likely possibility as long as rational citizens constitute the greater part of society and the legislature adequately represents these rational producers. For the rights due to any momentary minority are those due to all rational individuals; they are universal because they are rational, and the best earthly guarantee of rational decision making is a legislature representing the interests of rational people. Such people understand the purposes of government and know that it is not a device simply to inflict their will. Like a hammer, government may be subject to misuse, but its real functions are sufficiently obvious as to require a perverted will to misuse it.

The primary function of government is the protection of life and property. To this end, it must claim a monopoly of legitimate coercion; government would be powerless if all citizens claimed the right to enforce natural law as vigilantes. To guide the executive in the protection of property and the maintenance of order, the legislature must codify the law of nature into a system of criminal law and misdemeanors. Similarly, if the government is to fulfill its second obvious function, providing an impartial third party to settle disputes among private interests, it must provide a civil code of equity to guide those entrusted with the administration of justice. This, too, is largely a codification and elaboration of the law of nature, as understood and acknowledged by all reasonable individuals. Even if we disregard for the moment the practice of majority rule, a legislator would be foolhardy to let momentary considerations of short-term advantage take precedence over long-term interest in a rational administration of justice. For legislators are subject to the same civil and criminal laws as other citizens.

More vulnerable to abuse, perhaps, than providing security or maintaining a judicial system is the third and final function of government, which can be characterized as doing for people what they cannot do adequately by themselves. Since rational producers can do most things very well for themselves, this should not be an extensive field of governmental activity. Two appropriate policy areas have already been mentioned, namely, the establishment of a system of roads and a standardized currency. Others might be a postal system, regulation of broadcast airwaves, or a system of compulsory education. Regardless of the type of policy involved, it can be legitimate only if governmental intervention enhances the productive environment for all, however indirectly. For a government devoted to aiding only a segment of its population is precluded from claiming impartiality.

Another reason all governmental activity must be generally beneficial is that all functions of government invariably require taxation, which is an undeniable expropriation of property. Since the primary function of government focuses on the protection of property, not only must such expropriation be for a generally beneficial purpose, it must also gain the explicit consent of a majority of citizens. Governments can only tax those who enjoy the rights of citizenship, and these rights must include representation in the sovereign legislature. Moreover, the requirement of explicit consent would seem to necessitate, at a minimum, relatively frequent elections. Perhaps Locke had something less than this on his mind, but his logic is inevitably democratic, at least for those who own taxable property.

Locke's General Theory of Political Change and Stability

Revolutions happen not on every little mismanagement in public affairs. Great mistakes in the ruling part ... will be born by the people without ... murmur. But if a long train of abuses ... make the design visible to the people ..., it is not to be wondered that they should rouse themselves and endeavor ... [to] secure ... the ends for which government was at first erected.

—*The Second Treatise of Government*, chap. 19

The root cause of all political instability is irrationality, the neglect or ignorance of the self-evident principles of mutual accommodation. Susceptibility to political irrationality stems from both the inability to judge in one's own case and the failure to comprehend the appropriate functions of political authority. Although the former is the more frequent source of political contention and corruption, the latter is by far the more dangerous because it is more likely to lead to persecution and civil war.

As indicated in the preceding section, there are only three rational functions of government: protection, adjudication, and provision of essentially public services. All three enhance the productive endeavors of individuals. Yet Locke does not assume that productive endeavor necessarily is, or even should be, the highest priority of every individual. Some individuals become crazed with the quest for fame, others lose their individual sense of responsibility and reason through group identity. An irrational willingness to subordinate personal interests to those of an illusionary collectivity, combined with leaders intent on self-glorification, will inevitably lead to the persecution of those considered opponents, or even those considered merely complacent and unreliable. Property will be confiscated in the name of the cause, and force, rather than natural consensus, would provide the foundations for political power.

Yet the problem is more deep-seated than the existence of deranged and perverted people. For Locke never argues for the personal priority of the rationally self-evident, only for its political priority. Salvation, for instance, would appear to have a certain precedence over earthly prosperity and accomplishment. But both the belief in God and the atonement or ritual required for salvation are highly complex ideas. Theology, being a set of complex ideas, is not capable of conclusive proof, and only some form of suppression will lead to theological consensus. If one were to hold that personal and political priorities must coincide, once again force, rather than natural consensus, would provide the foundations for political power.

Force, however, cannot effectively substitute for reason as the basis for political order. As underscored by Hobbes, fear is as likely to lead to aggression as to acquiescence. Moreover, in a social context the use of force itself requires concerted action and mutual trust among those who wield it. Only reason can provide a sure foundation for trust, but only reason working with relatively simple ideas, close to the daily experience of all human beings. If, therefore, individuals wish to live, worship, and wonder in peace, they must, to borrow a Christian metaphor, let others burn in eternal hell. In other words, they must confine the legitimate field of political authority to the mundane things about which all rational people can agree and tolerate diversity, even idiocy, about more important matters. In a rational polity, everybody must have the right to be wrong.

Yet nobody has the right to judge in his or her own case, and when somebody does, the likely result is corruption, tyranny, and discord. As previously discussed, majority rule is required to prevent self-interested parties from being able to disregard the long-term interests of all in favor of short-term personal advantage. Obviously, if a majority of citizens is biased by self-interest, the principle of majority rule cannot procure an impartial arbiter. The majority then becomes, to use James Madison's terms, a "faction," and in a representative democracy it would be the "most dangerous faction" just because of the principle of majority rule. This is a particularly insidious prospect, since important issues of public policy frequently divide whole populations along neat lines of self-interest, and since populations, like individuals, are susceptible to this sort of temporary irrationality.

Locke gives no evidence of having anticipated this rather likely possibility. Fortunately, however, the arguments put forth by Madison in *The Federalist Papers* provide a plausible explanation of how to have majority rule while avoiding rule by a majority faction. In brief, Madison proposes that a factional majority would be difficult to maintain in large, complex societies because the diversity of interests would require much compromising to occur before they could be combined into a majority faction. No one likes to compromise, and the more compromising required to form a coalition, the less stable the coalition will be. In the face of a constitutional structure characterized by checks and balances, where a majority must be strong and persistent to unify the three branches of government, a large faction is likely to be ineffective. It simply would not last long enough. Majorities of sufficient strength and coherence are likely to rest on the rational, long-term interests of all citizens. By compromising the sovereignty of the legislature with a system of checks and balances, the principle of majority rule is reaffirmed.

All of which is fine in those few societies where this sort of institutional tinkering is possible. In most societies, it is not. Political power is often independent of majority sentiments, and, in any event, majorities in many countries are consistently supportive of policies redistributing property or suppressing unpopular ideas. What is to be done in the face of the tyranny of the irrational?

In the case of a dictator or distinct political elite, including a wayward legislature, Locke forthrightly declares the right of popular revolution. Actually, in such instances it is not the people who rebel against authority, but those who have irrationally claimed authority who rebel against the people. In regimes providing genuine and frequent opportunities for citizens to elect representatives, such usurpation is highly unlikely and revolution almost never necessary. Even in regimes lacking effective electoral machinery, popular rebellion against irrational and unjust government will be infrequent. This is not because rulers in authoritarian regimes can be relied on to act responsibly, but because of the reluctance of rational individuals to disrupt their lives and engage in politics. Both prudence and personal priorities disincline rational producers from devoting themselves to public affairs. Government is an unfortunate necessity, and public service no more than a duty and a burden. Consequently, acknowledging the right of revolution does not threaten public order, and when popular revolutions occur, they are invariably justified.

More difficult is a situation characterized by irrational majorities, rather than irrational rulers, where rational individuals understanding the proper functions of government are in a minority. For despite the self-evident reasonableness of natural law, great masses of the world's population have difficulty applying the common-sense rationality of daily life to public affairs. Claims they would never make of their neighbors they often demand from different classes, geographical sections, or ethnic groups. Differences in religion or lifestyle that would be a breech of etiquette even to mention in polite society become publicly intolerable in the collective abstract. Popular sentiments often support arbitrary confiscation of property and suppression of unpopular belief.

In these circumstances, it might seem that rational government would require that the rights of citizenship be confined to those able to act rationally on them and that a rebellion against an irrational popular government may be as justified as one against a tyrannical dictator. Such cannot be the case. For no person or distinct group can judge its own case, and the political irrationality of a clique of rational producers cannot be much different from that of the inconsistent masses. Indeed, the latter has the advantage of being popular, making force less likely.

Majority rule is not simply a pragmatic decision-making procedure; it is the instrument by which we are able to overcome our own limitations. It works, however, only when we are making decisions for ourselves, rather than for others. If a large proportion of the population, through poverty or tradition, cannot be helped by this instrument, then Liberal democracy is not an option, and the minority of rational individuals cannot claim a monopoly of citizenship rights. To exercise power as a class would undermine the very rationality on which such a claim would rest.

Barring emigration, there are only two options for the rational individual in a predominately irrational society. The first is to turn inward, to be as productive as circumstances allow, prudently accommodating oneself to the limitations imposed by a less than ideal environment. The other is to recognize that rights cannot be fully enjoyed unless enjoyed by all and to work to create a society in which all can hope to realize their productive potential and acknowledge their mutual rights. It is self-evident that the two options are not mutually exclusive and could be pursued simultaneously.

The Politics of Rights

Although under most circumstances a parliamentary regime is to be preferred, a rational person should be able to abide a wide range of political arrangements. After all, politics is not a very meaningful form of activity. Truly fulfilling experience is to be found in private endeavor, rather than in public service. One performs one's public duty not because this is the path to glory or happiness but simply from a combination of prudence and moral obligation.

Constant prudence is required to ensure that government remains restricted to its limited ends, that it not encroach on the individual rights it is intended to protect. Yet a sense of moral responsibility is also essential. For the normal routine of politics in a rational society involves resolving disputes among private interests. The temptation to advance private interests over those shared by all rational producers is necessarily great given the importance of personal property to the individual. If humans are as Locke believes, citizenship, like government itself, is an unfortunate but necessary burden.

A Brief Guide to the Literature

For a readable account of Locke's life, with special attention to his political activity, one could not do better than Maurice Cranston's *John Locke: A Biography* (1957). Peter Laslett's "Introduction" to his edition of Locke's *Two Treatises of Government* (1963) convincingly demonstrates that the all-important "Second Treatise" was originally written to enlist support for a patently illegal plot to deny James II his rightful succession to the throne. Before Laslett's historical sleuthing, it was widely believed that the purpose of the essay was to justify, after the fact, the Glorious Revolution. It is now generally accepted that the essay was intended to be a call to revolution, rather than a justification of the status quo.

Nonetheless, a number of influential interpreters have argued that

Locke's thought has authoritarian conclusions almost as severe as that of Hobbes. Willmore Kendall, in *John Locke and the Doctrine of Majority-Rule* (1941), and Leo Strauss, in *Natural Right and History* (1953), claim that Locke rejects any meaningful notion of natural law and that once an individual has consented to be part of political society, he or she has forever agreed to acquiesce to the will of the sovereign majority. By this interpretation, Locke justifies neither individual rights nor constitutional limits on governmental authority. Whatever the majority decides is rational defines the extent of its legislative jurisdiction.

Kendall and Strauss were conservative critics of Liberal individualism, maintaining that the creed of the self-interested, socially autonomous individual logically leads to a dictatorial majority, rather than limited government tolerant of individual diversity. Paradoxically, much the same conclusion has been reached by many politically radical critics of Liberal individualism. In his influential work *The Political Theory of Possessive Individualism* (1964), C.B. Macpherson cogently argues that since the chief end of government is the protection of property, only those with substantial property can claim political rights in Locke's scheme of things. Consequently, it is not just any majority that has the right to rule, but only a majority of the propertied class. Moreover, since protection of property is the chief end of government, this end takes legal priority over any other rights individuals might claim. For Macpherson, Locke is nothing more than an apologist for the power of a capitalist elite.

Although Strauss and Macpherson each believed that he had discovered Locke's true intention, the challenging nature of their interpretations stems from their ability to explain certain apparent inconsistencies in his writings. In other words, their claims of historical validity are largely irrelevant to the real value of their interpretations. In fact, according to John Dunn's analysis, in *The Political Thought of John Locke: An Historical Account of the Argument of the "Two Treatises of Government"* (1969), given Locke's religious convictions, he could not have personally sanctioned unrestrained majority rule of either the popular or class variety. The seeming inconsistencies of his thought disappear when seen in the context of his time and cultural context.

From a social scientific perspective, of course, if a system of thought makes sense only in the context of its author's time, it is not likely to have much relevance to an understanding of ours. Yet the interpretations of Strauss and Macpherson are also of limited relevance to social science because neither results in a viable conceptual alternative. Strauss and Macpherson are philosophical critics of Liberal individualism, attempting to demonstrate that such a position logically entails either mob rule or class rule, rather than a constitutionally limited regime protective of individual rights. In both cases the intent is to call into question Liberal individualism, rather than provide an enhanced understanding of how such principles might be realized. For an interpretation that attempts to read Locke as a logically coherent Liberal individualist, see the excellent study by Ruth Grant, *John Locke's Liberalism* (1987). More recently, in *The Anxiety of Freedom: Imagination and Individuality in Locke's Political Thought* (1992), Uday Singh Mehta has offered a provocative analysis of the uncertain psychological underpinnings of Locke's prescriptive individualism.

Rousseau and the
Politics of Citizenship

The Historical Rousseau

Born in the independent Swiss city of Geneva in 1712, Jean-Jacques Rousseau took pride in his status as a citizen of Geneva and occasionally glorified its civic virtues. In reality, he left his native city at the age of sixteen, and there is not much concrete evidence of his ever really wanting to return for anything more than a rare visit. There was little in the way of family or happy memories to bind him to his birthplace when he left, and he never established ties with any other political community in subsequent years. A footloose vagabond during much of his youth, successively a social climber, a nonconformist, and a social critic in his maturity, and finally in his last years an outcast, Rousseau was always an outsider.

He was an infant when his mother died. His father, a watchmaker, was an insubstantial personality who, when Rousseau was still a young boy, had to flee Geneva to avoid prosecution for brawling. Although he maintained contact with his father, Rousseau was eventually apprenticed, first to a lawyer and then to an engraver. He was too unruly and irresponsible to make a good apprentice and suffered accordingly. Locked out of the city one evening because he failed to return before the gates had been closed, and knowing from previous experience that this would mean punishment, he struck out on his own.

His experiences as a rootless youth need not be detailed. Converting to Catholicism after leaving Switzerland, he became part of the entourage of a financially comfortable woman, also a Swiss convert, who provided him with a secure base. In her household he was able to expand on the rudiments of education he had earlier received from his father and his mother's relatives. He especially excelled in music, which his patronness hoped would provide him with a career. He repaid her kindness by providing amusement and affection, but this mutually beneficial arrangement was by its very nature temporary. Almost thirty, Rousseau departed from his benefactor's house for the last time, determined to make his mark. After serving as a tutor to an influential family in Lyon, he was inevitably drawn to the cultural capital of Paris.

By virtue of his talents as a musician, he achieved a limited success and became an acquaintance of some of the notable figures of the Enlightenment. He even secured a position as secretary to the French ambassador to Venice, but had to return to Paris after arguing with his superior. He became increasing alienated from the conventions of Parisian society, increasingly prone to nonconformist behavior in his personal habits. His alienation from society was given literary expression in a prize-winning essay in which he argued that the advance of the arts and sciences had a detrimental effect on morality.

With this essay, in addition to a very popular opera, Rousseau became a well-known literary figure, and almost all his subsequent work assumes a critical stance toward existing societies, especially Parisian society. This stance is best developed in his brilliant essay, "Discourse on the Origin and Foundations of Inequality among Men." This second essay and *The Social Contract* are the most important expositions of the political implications of Rousseau's thought. His other important works can perhaps best be understood as attempts to discern how it might be possible to be moral in the midst of an immoral social context. Only in *The Social Contract* did he attempt to explicate the general principles of a rational political community in which morality and citizenship could be combined.

Rousseau himself never enjoyed the benefits of such citizenship. Indeed, for many years he was a fugitive from the persecution of governments that considered his social and religious ideas subversive. Moreover, there is good reason to question whether he consistently lived up to his own moral standard in his personal conduct. Perhaps this is reason to give more serious attention than he apparently did to the possibility that moral freedom requires the civic commitment that defines the citizen.

Human Nature and Rational Motivation

To renounce liberty is to renounce being a man, to surrender the rights of humanity and even its duties.... Such a renunciation is incompatible with man's nature; to remove all liberty from his will is to remove all morality from his acts.

—*The Social Contract*, bk. I, chap. 4

Like Hobbes and Locke before him, Rousseau was a contract theorist who resorted to the intellectual construction of a hypothetical "state of nature." But, unlike Hobbes, he did not define it as the condition toward which our action will take us when we cannot rely on authority, and therefore always a possibility; and, unlike Locke, he did not use the device to discern the principles of legitimacy that rational individuals would adopt in creating a political authority. Instead, Rousseau used the state-of-nature construct to demonstrate that humans can be human only in a social context, that without mutual obligations, we would not be creatures worthy of respect.

Extrapolating from humans as we now see them, Rousseau asks us to imagine what they would be like if they had been born in an environment lacking not just government but all social institutions. Locke's state of nature is unbelievable, from Rousseau's perspective, because those who inhabit it are civilized beings with such social institutions as stable families and language. Rousseau takes it as an anthropological fact that patterns of authority would be one of the earliest social institutions to evolve, and the individuals who eventually come together to create a rationally legitimate government through contract could not be completely ignorant of the deficiencies of irrational political and social institutions.

In a believable state of nature human beings would not be distinguishable in any significant way from other mammals. We would be, in other words, dumb brutes. We could not make use of our large brains because we would lack language, a symbolic code that serves as an index to the contents of our memories, just as a card catalogue allows researchers to make use of the contents of a very large library. Just like Hobbes, Rousseau argued that conscious deliberation required language. But language would develop only when there was a need to communicate, which means it would develop only in a social context. Consequently, the mental advantage we would have over other mammals would be slight in the state of nature.

If we assume a good environment, with temperate climate, adequate food, and the absence of predators, we would live happy lives in the state of nature. Our needs would be simple, almost solely physiological, and in a good environment easily satisfied. Whatever differences in physical attributes we might have, without the mental equipment to build cages or set rules, they could not lead to domination. We would be essentially equal and naturally free, obeying only our natural inclinations. We would, from the perspective of our present development, be nice animals. We lack fangs, our fingernails could not serve as claws, and we are neither territorial nor particularly aggressive. All in all, with our large brains and our mild dispositions, we would make excellent pets.

However fond we feel toward our dogs and cats, we do not respect them, and there would be no reason to respect what we would be in this hypothetical state of nature. For we would not be human, but only potentially human. What do we have, which our pets do not share, that allows us to recognize one another as mature human beings worthy of respect? Clearly it is not the mere ability to communicate, any more than it is the machinelike ability to calculate. It is, rather, the ability to judge, oneself as well as others. This requires that the individual set a standard and organize his or her actions according to this standard. We are human only to the extent that we are free moral agents, acting in accordance with what we think is right. Mature humans need justification and self-respect, and such creatures can develop and fulfill their human potential only in a social environment.

The Motivational Basis of Social Solidarity

This universal desire for reputation, honors, and advancement ... exercises and holds up to comparison our faculties and powers.... It is to ... this unremitting rage of distinguishing ourselves, that we owe the best and the worst things we possess ...; that is to say, a great many bad things, and a very few good ones.
—*Discourse on the Origin and Foundations of Inequality*, pt. II

Although the primary motives in human affairs are self-respect and justification, these motives develop only in a social context and therefore cannot explain the original establishment of social ties. Only practical necessity would have forced dumb brutes into sufficient proximity to allow the development of their human potential. Rousseau provides a hypothetical anthropology to indicate how civilization might have developed from his hypothetical state of nature. It is a useful exercise, not because it tells us how civilization actually evolved, but because it discloses the psychic incentives that lead individuals to take social obligations seriously, as well as the psychic costs of their doing so. We can learn more from Rousseau about the psychology of social solidarity than its anthropology.

A change in climate would suffice to force the inhabitants of the state of nature to seek shelter. Not possessing the mental equipment required for construction, only those finding natural shelter, such as a cave, would survive, and larger caves would eventually house a number of the brutes. In close proximity the rudiments of language naturally would begin to develop. The increased difficulties of satisfying basic requirements would eventually lead to cooperation and a primitive sense of community among the cave dwellers. If the march of civilization could be stopped, it would be best to stop it here. Needs still would be simple, and despite the increased effort required in a less than ideal climate, they still could be satisfied. Moreover, individuals would be enjoying one another's company, and each would feel part of the community. But civilization cannot be stopped. For one thing, we will not allow it; the whole purpose of the hypothetical anthropology is to disclose the psychological underpinnings of contemporary societies. More important, this idyllic primitive community would have to change, for it is psychologically untenable. Inevitably, a new need would arise, a need so strong that it dominates all others. Furthermore, this new need, which can arise only in a social setting, provides a powerful motive for social solidarity as well as the driving force behind the advance of civilization.

To understand this need, picture our primitive cave community at the end of the working day, gathered around the cave fire to enjoy one another's company. Primitive entertainment relies more on mimicry and parody than subtle wordplay or punch lines, and we can imagine that one of their number has a special knack for humorous characterization. These nightly gatherings are the most pleasurable moments of the day, and the climax of the evening is when the talented one is induced to perform. One morning, the great entertainer announces that he or she cannot join the daily hunt for food if the group expects quality entertainment in the evening. Special talent requires special treatment.

⚹ In this hypothetical context, such a claim would be revolutionary. It implies that the talented are more deserving than the untalented. However dimly, these primitives would detect that their colleague thinks himself or herself more worthy than they. This realization suggests an unacceptable possibility: Perhaps their colleague is correct, perhaps they are less worthy. The possibility is profoundly disturbing, a source of extreme anxiety. Self-consciousness is born, the age of innocence terminated. Each is now condemned to proving his or her own worth. The need for *self-esteem* pervades all action, and even basic physiological needs are subordinated to it. Indeed, people are now often willing to risk their lives for the sake of honor and reputation.

It would be a mistake, however, to conclude that such people are now equipped to find happiness by living fulfilling, human lives. Exactly the opposite is the case. We become self-conscious through comparison with others, and we attempt to satisfy the resulting need for self-esteem through invidious comparison. Because we bolster our own egos at the expense of others, our self-esteem rests on reputation, rather than an independent sense of worth. And because the need for self-esteem is manifested as the quest for social status, it is a need that can never be satisfied. For social status is always relative and therefore never secure. Having a need that can never be satisfied is almost the definition of misery, and whether acknowledged or not, self-consciousness more frequently leads to dissatisfaction and anxiety than happiness and fulfillment.

For this very reason, it also leads to civilization. Tormented by the anxiety of self-doubt, one attempts to distinguish oneself as best one can. When talent and opportunity combine, the quest for social distinction provides the incentive to create, to build, or to subdue. The stage is set for progress in science, art, and industry. More germane to the political theorist, however, is that the quest for social status provides foundations for social solidarity by rendering individuals radically dependent on their social context.

Social dependence results from a number of causes, the most obvious of which are economic. A high degree of division of labor combined with an unequal distribution of property compel most individuals to conform to the expectations of others. Still, these economic relations are more likely to be seen as fetters than benefits, and by themselves would be more likely to be a source of social discord than social solidarity. Economic considerations are less important than those of status, however. Except for the destitute, in fact, economic advantages are important primarily because they are conventional signs of social standing. Wealthy people buy mansions with huge front lawns, large cars with an excessive amount of chrome, or fine jewelry, not because front lawns, chrome, or diamonds are useful or enjoyable in themselves, but because these things are, at least in our culture, symbols of success and status.

Status is all important, and to exist status must be stratified. To value status, therefore, is to affirm social inequality. Contemporary societies are intricate pyramids of status, supported even by those at the lower levels, if not the lowest, because even modest status is important to those who must try to achieve self-esteem through invidious comparison. Simply put, the quest for social status results in social solidarity because social conventions and symbols are essential to social status. To put it so simply, however, fails to indicate the severity of the social dependence that follows from the motivational priority of status. For the individual depends on society not just for providing the means to what is wanted but even for what is wanted. When social status is the ultimate end, then society dictates what is worthy of esteem. Instead of free moral agents, individuals become superficial panderers to prevailing opinion, driven by fad and fashion. Social solidarity is achieved at the expense of human development, and contemporary societies are more likely to foster moral monsters than free moral agents.

The Function and Organization of Authority

What man loses by the social contract is his natural liberty and an unlimited right to everything ... he succeeds in getting; what he gains is civil liberty and the proprietorship of all he possesses.... We might ... add, to what man acquires in the civil state, moral liberty, which alone makes him truly master of himself; for ... obedience to a law which we prescribe to ourselves is liberty.

—*The Social Contract*, bk. I, chap. 8

Society can be as much a threat to our humanity as a condition for its realization. Rousseau's political thought can be seen as an attempt to remove the threat and retain the condition. His social contract is entered into by rational individuals attempting to create a community that would help them live up to their human potential. They would not be worried about the deficiencies of a state of nature, but those of irrational society. The only way to resolve them, according to Rousseau, is to create a political authority devoted to the task. Yet this raises a seemingly impossible dilemma. If humanity is defined in terms of free moral agency, how could it ever be reconciled with the existence of a higher, political authority? It would seem that authority necessarily limits individual autonomy, moral or otherwise.

To reconcile moral freedom with civic commitment, rational individuals must create a moral community of which each is an indivisible part. The creation of such a community requires two commitments. First, each must agree to place the good of the community above his or her own particular good. Second, all citizens must participate in determining what constitutes the public good, and none shall be eligible for special recognition of any kind. The second commitment, in other words, is to complete political equality. Together, these commitments create a social environment incompatible with the quest for social status, replacing personal pride with civic pride.

The first commitment literally creates the community. For a community, as opposed to an organization or association, is a group in which the members are committed to one another just because they are members of the group. Each member is willing to sacrifice personal advantage in order to strengthen a community because the group itself is meaningful. To illustrate, consider two groups, a local chapter of the PTA (Parent-Teacher Association) and a family. The latter is almost certainly a community, while the PTA is not likely to qualify. A family is a community, not because its members might have strong affective attachments to one another, but because members feel obliged to do whatever is necessary to keep it together, irrespective of personal sacrifice. When members no longer feel this obligation, they are a family only in the legal or biological senses of the term. The members of a PTA, in contrast, join only because membership is advantageous to either themselves or a family member. The PTA is likely to mean nothing in itself, and if a large portion of its members decide that it fails to provide the promised benefits that led them to participate, they will drop out and the PTA will cease to function.

Every true community rests on the individual commitment to the group's survival. In Rousseau's terminology, every community rests on a *general will* toward the good of the group. Only the existence of such a general will makes sense of the terms "public" and "the public good." When rational individuals commit themselves to being citizens of a political community, they all commit themselves to the same thing. Their general will is to maximize the public good, which is the community's strength and survival. Since the community is constituted by the commitment of the citizens, what ultimately is in the public good is whatever maintains and strengthens the commitment that citizens make toward one another. As long as a community exists, then by definition a general will toward its good exists, and the criterion of the public good is always the strengthening of the general will itself.

In order to reconcile communal commitment with moral autonomy, however, the second condition is essential. Every citizen must participate in determining what is in the public good. By definition, all true citizens want the same thing, for a common commitment to the community is what makes them citizens. Citizens may disagree over how to achieve the end, but they cannot differ over the end itself. With sufficient deliberation, therefore, they should be able to arrive at a consensus on the best means to achieve the common end. Consequently, to the extent that all are able to participate in determining what is in the public good, then any decision reached by the citizens will be in accord with what each of them wants. Obeying laws arrived at through deliberation and consensus cannot be an imposition. The citizen is simply obeying a law that he or she prescribed for all, including himself or herself. Obeying a law that one prescribes for oneself is civic freedom, as well as the very definition of a free moral agent. The activity of the free citizen is the distinctly human activity, and one develops one's human potential through civic commitment and public responsibility.

Political equality requires both that the legislative authority rest solely with the citizens deliberating as a collective body and that all legislation apply generally to all citizens, rather than specifically to one or a portion of them. Obviously, even a general law will affect some more than others, but if citizens are to obey only laws prescribed by themselves, each must be an indivisible part of a collective body. None can be singled out for special treatment of either a favorable or pejorative nature. The reconciliation of collective authority and individual autonomy rests on the commitment to the public good, which in the last analysis is no more than a commitment to strengthen the general commitment that creates the public. By definition, then, neither favoritism nor persecution is compatible with the general will of all true citizens.

For this reason, however, the sovereign citizens cannot collectively administer or enforce legislation. Laws must be general rules, but the application of a general rule requires one to deal with particular cases, to single out those citizens who must be constrained to observe their acknowledged public responsibilities. Consequently, the executive power enforcing the law must be a distinct agency, entrusted to civil magistrates acting in the public's name but exercising no legislative power of their own. This executive power, which Rousseau refers to simply as the "government," serves as an essential intermediary between the active, legislating public, which Rousseau calls the "sovereign," and the same public at all other times, which Rousseau calls the "state." We are "citizens" when engaged in public affairs and "subjects" when living in accordance with the public will. The government's function is to ensure that subjects, when pursuing their particular interests in the course of daily life, conform to the requirements of the public good as they have determined them in their role as citizens.

In a rational political system, then, there must be two very different forms of public activity. The first is deliberative and consists of an effort to respond to the difficulties and challenges facing a political community in such a manner as to foster and maintain a high degree of civic commitment among the citizens. This form must involve all citizens. The other form of public activity involves primarily public officials, those employed to represent and serve the community. This activity might be characterized as "operative." Those entrusted with the administration of public affairs should be attempting to apply the considered will of the community not only to forgetful or irresolute citizens but also to the unforeseen exigencies and vagaries of a shifting environment. How a political community might be organized to ensure that these two forms of public activity are accomplished and kept distinct would, of course, vary with circumstances. There is little reason to consider such questions in the present context, however, because in actual practice it is almost impossible to keep them distinct or to preserve the sovereignty of the citizens over those entrusted with the power of government.

Rousseau's General Theory of Political Change and Stability

When . . . the meanest interest brazenly lays hold of the sacred name of "public good" . . ., and iniquitous decrees directed solely to private interest get passed under the name of laws . . ., does it follow that the general will is exterminated or corrupted? Not at all: it is always constant, unalterable, and pure; but it is subordinated to other wills which encroach on its sphere.

—*The Social Contract*, bk. IV, chap. 1

We encounter something new with Rousseau. Irrational relationships that make us miserable may contribute as much to political stability as rational arrangements, those which facilitate fulfilling, human activity. As previously indicated, social solidarity in most existing societies, by Rousseau's analysis, results in large part from the need for social status. This need can never really be satisfied, and for this reason those driven by it are necessarily insecure and anxious. Yet their very anxiety will reinforce their aversion to social criticism and their distrust of social reform. This is because the need for social status renders the individual dependent on his or her social context. Society determines what is worthy of esteem and provides the symbolic marks of distinction essential for the validation of personal status. For a person who needs the approval of others, the more uncertain such approval seems, the more doggedly will it be pursued. By implication, those at the lower levels of the pyramid of status can be expected to be almost as concerned with social order as those at the top.

Dependence of the insecure on approval of their social superiors, as well as the gratification they receive from whatever sense of superiority they can feel over those of even less status, is only one reason for the often noted conservatism of the socially disadvantaged. Another is the traditionalism typical of those who consider themselves a "people." For however unlikely Rousseau's ideal of a perfectly egalitarian community ruled by active citizens, a strong sense of community is an almost ubiquitous aspect of social reality. People have always been ready to sacrifice themselves for their village or tribe, and in the last few centuries millions have done so for their nation. In modern mass societies, with highly literate and easily mobilized citizens, few regimes could survive on their own without the widespread conviction that they represent in some way the collective interests of a national community.

There are, then, two primary sources of social and political stability: the sense of patriotism derived from identification with a political community, and the sense of individual distinction derived from social status. Both sources of stability are probably indispensable in modern nation-states, but each is also a source of instability. Moreover, each tends to be corrosive of the other in that an exaggerated concern for personal distinction will rationalize social duty only when it brings social honor, and an intense commitment to community renders any claim of personal distinction self-indulgent and selfish. Before discussing the implications of this mutually deleterious relationship, however, it is important to understand how each of these sources of stability can be a source of instability as well.

In itself, communal commitment, defined as the willingness of the individual to sacrifice personal needs and wants for those of the group, cannot be a major source of instability. Apart from disagreement over community needs, which should not lead to conflict if the mutual commitment of all members is acknowledged, the major problem is the proliferation of communities. In fact, every group tends to develop a "group will" in that the group becomes a value in itself to at least some of its members. Even groups joined in order to achieve specific benefits, such as a labor union or the company by which one is employed, often become so important to the member as to obscure their initial, instrumental purpose. Indeed, in the past some have killed and died for their union, and many business corporations expect and receive lifelong loyalty and remarkable sacrifice from their career employees.

Proliferation of communities can result in social and political instability because it leads to divided loyalties. This is sufficiently obvious as to require little elaboration. Regimes in societies characterized by diverse ethnic, religious, regional, or class identities are more prone to political disunity than those that are not. From Rousseau's perspective, however, all political communities, no matter how homogeneous their populations, are plagued with a divided loyalty of a particularly pernicious sort.

For the government itself is a distinct group, and it is almost inevitable that those participating in what I earlier called the operative dimension of public life will seek to evade control of the larger community in order to facilitate their work and perpetuate their authority. This would be a strong tendency even in a community approximating Rousseau's ideal, where it would be accepted that only the people have the right to legislate. In existing electoral systems, where government legislates in the name of an elusive if not illusionary popular will, a high degree of governmental autonomy is likely to be the rule. If this autonomy is widely perceived, these governments are likely to face chronic problems in obtaining the voluntary compliance essential for effective administration.

Few such governments, however, will be completely successful in suppressing public recognition of their autonomy from community control. This is because of the defects inherent in the other source of stability. For although the need for social status renders individuals dependent on their social context, it does so at the cost of interpersonal competition. Generally, such rivalry will impede social cooperation and will make the administration of public programs more difficult. A more decisive threat to political stability will be rivalry and distrust among the politically powerful. At a minimum, their competition for personal distinction will lead opposing factions to make mutual recriminations concerning one another's fidelity to the public interest. Widespread cynicism and distrust of political authority is the likely consequence, reducing the probability that any faction could achieve sufficient popular support to secure its position. Because the need for personal distinction, rather than Hobbesian fear, is the driving motive, any apparent vulnerability of those who control the primary symbols of status inevitably will generate challenges from those who wish to replace them.

Such are the fundamental causes of political disorder. Popular disaffection and the egotistic contentiousness of elites will undermine the effectiveness and stability of regimes even in societies without serious ethnic, religious, or class divisions. Since these fundamental sources of instability are derived from the same need for self-respect as those of social solidarity, they cannot be eradicated. Of course their effects can be curtailed by propaganda and intimidation, but such expedients rarely provide more than temporary or partial security for those who rule.

To the extent that they are effective, however, both official propaganda and intimidation clearly are detrimental to genuine citizenship and popular rule. Perhaps for this reason, Rousseau was not particularly concerned with the inherent problems of political order in modern societies. For him, the realistic options for human development lay primarily in the nonpolitical spheres of experience—of one's family, one's friends, and, for those fortunate enough to be born into a relatively rustic social environment, one's village. At best, he only hints at a process by which both regime stability and citizenship might be enhanced in the large, complex nation-states in which we live. Nevertheless, from a social scientific perspective, an assessment of rational political potential is a principal contribution that political theory makes to political science, and we need to explore the implications of Rousseau's political thought for a rational politics in modern societies.

In light of the huge gap between his ideal model of a participatory democracy and almost all existing regimes, Rousseau concluded that the ideal could be approximated only in a small society. Nevertheless, he also recognized that many, perhaps most, political societies are communities; the great majority of their members do not enjoy the active political life of citizens, but their patriotism and willingness to sacrifice for their nation is a clear indication of a sense of community. The general will may be "mute" because the people do not exercise sovereignty, but the general will exists because the people feel themselves part of a collective entity. They are "subjects," rather than "citizens."

Population size, the authority of experts in an age of advanced technology, and the political power of organized economic interests all conspire to limit the political involvement and consciousness of subjects in modern political societies. Moreover, as Rousseau also observed, those who constitute the governing stratum of society develop a group will of their own and attempt to discourage the active involvement of "outsiders" in public affairs. Whether wittingly or not, they usurp the legislative power of the community. And whether sincerely or not, they claim to be acting according to both the public interest and the public will. As discussed in preceding paragraphs, governing elites must claim this because popular patriotism is one of the conditions of political stability and effectiveness in modern societies.

From Rousseau's perspective, the greatest threat to the real public interest in almost all existing political communities is pervasive political inequality, for this enables governing elites to usurp the legislative power of the people and negates the legislative relevance of the general will. Even in small political communities approximating his ideal, Rousseau recognized that the major concern of most legislation would have to be the removal of impediments to equal political participation. In states where legislative power has been almost completely usurped by a distinct stratum of the population, however, political equality will not be a high priority. For despite the likelihood that political contenders will routinely question one another's commitment to the public interest, as long as they are motivated primarily by the maintenance of their own status, the neglect of the paramount threat to the public interest will never be among their mutual criticisms.

Yet if the general will that creates the community exists, as attested by the willingness of the mass of citizens to sacrifice personal interests for the sake of the state just because they are a "people," then citizenship itself can be an important political issue. This is especially true in regimes legitimated by democratic ideals and characterized by open competition. To use a term unfamiliar to Rousseau, a *populist* politics of political equality, supported by animosity against "special interests" and privileged elites, is a realistic possibility. The general cynicism toward governing elites, due in part to the mutual criticism of contending politicians, works to the advantage of those who champion the active involvement of citizens in public affairs. While all politicians will claim to represent the public interest, only those sincerely committed to popular citizenship are likely to expose and demand the elimination of patterns of political inequality.

Many contingencies, obviously, will determine whether such champions of the people are able to gain political influence or whether entrenched elites are able to brand them as dangerous demagogues. Yet, however successful they are politically, it is just as obvious that their ability to involve fellow citizens in the determination of public policy will be, at best, limited. The nature of the modern nation-state foreordains that the realization of Rousseau's ideal could only be partial. But citizenship can be a matter of degree, and there is little justification for dismissing an ideal as irrelevant because of the difficulty of approximating it. And from a purely practical viewpoint, to disregard the ideal of citizenship might be very hazardous. For if Rousseau has correctly discerned the mainsprings of human motivation, every political regime needs a politics of citizenship to restore periodically the priority of commitment to the "people" over that of short-term personal advantage. Otherwise, governments would have to rely on appeals to self-interest, propaganda, and intimidation. To place much faith in these devices in order to rule a population that had lost all sense of civic commitment would be truly utopian.

The Politics of Citizenship

When considering public affairs, the perfect citizen would be concerned solely with the public good, irrespective of the consequences for his or her particular circumstances. All things being equal, this may seem an ideal unlikely to be realized except in small communities characterized by frequent face-to-face interaction. Yet all things, and all people, are rarely equal. Under most circumstances, the greatest threat to the public good is political inequality. Political equality is an essential condition of citizenship, and citizenship is not only an essential component of the public good but also relates to the highest of all individual interests. To be a free moral agent, a human being, is to follow laws we affirm for ourselves, rather than laws imposed by others.

To the extent citizens recognize the connection between political equality and personal freedom, they will be ready to sacrifice personal convenience and comfort, and perhaps life itself, in order to diminish this ever-present threat to the public interest. Even in modern nation-states the personal stake each has in the realization of the public good is felt by all except those poor souls driven by the need to distinguish themselves from their compatriots, or those for whom citizenship is nothing more than an insurance policy.

A Brief Guide to the Literature

No other important political thinker has provoked such varied interpretations as Rousseau. Moreover, none of these interpretations has been generally acknowledged as the standard; in the understanding of Rousseau's thought, there is no orthodoxy. Fortunately, there is a firm consensus on which biography of the man is best, even though its third, concluding volume has not yet been published. Maurice Cranston's *Jean-Jacques: The Early Life and Work of Jean-Jacques Rousseau, 1712–1754* (1982) and *The Noble Savage: Jean-Jacques Rousseau, 1754–1762* (1991) are essential preparatory reading for any serious investigation into Rousseau's work. For a broad overview of Rousseau's thought, one could certainly do worse than Ronald Grimsley's *The Philosophy of Rousseau* (1973), although some would disagree even with this cautious endorsement.

The extent of divergence in the assessment of Rousseau is indicated by the title of John W. Chapman's book, *Rousseau—Totalitarian or Liberal?* (1956). Chapman's answer is that Rousseau is, ultimately, a liberal, which is also the answer given in Alfred Cobban's well-known survey of Rousseau's political thought, *Rousseau and the Modern State* (1934). J.L. Talmon, in *The Rise of Totalitarian Democracy* (1952), is the most famous of those who have reached the opposite conclusion. Yet very few recent commentators believe that Rousseau was either a liberal or a totalitarian. Some, best represented by Judith N. Shklar, *Men and Citizens: A Study of Rousseau's Social Theory* (1969), paint a picture of a backward-looking, pessimistic, and apolitical moralist. For others, well represented by James Miller, *Rousseau: Dreamer of Democracy* (1984), Rousseau is a visionary of an ideal participant democracy.

To some extent the challenge of seeing unity behind the diversity of

Rousseau's major writings, combined with his own insistence that such a unity exists, has encouraged interpretive strategies aimed at deriving what I have called conceptual paradigms from Rousseau's work. Each interpreter, of course, claims to have isolated the "real" Rousseau. From a social scientific perspective, such claims are of no more than secondary importance. The really important question is which of these Rousseaus is best able to provide us with a coherent political outlook. From this perspective, two works can be highly recommended, Ernst Cassirer, *The Question of Jean-Jacques Rousseau* (1963), and Arthur M. Melzer, *The Natural Goodness of Man: On the System of Rousseau's Thought* (1990). For those interested in what Rousseau "really" thought and felt, Melzer is probably closer to the mark. Cassirer's Rousseau, however, suffers fewer ambiguities.

{ 10 }

Mill and the
Politics of Character

The Historical Mill

John Stuart Mill's life paralleled the consolidation of the industrial revolution and the rise of England as the greatest imperial power on earth. Born in London in 1806, Mill shared the Victorian faith in progress. He did not share, however, the middle-class complacency of his age. Instead, he was a reformer who championed the expansion of voting rights, the public provision of social services, and the rights of women.

Yet there is a tension between elitism and democracy in the thought of John Stuart Mill, a tension perhaps embedded in his early youth and training. His father, James Mill, was a close associate of Jeremy Bentham, founder of the philosophical position known as Utilitarianism. Bentham argued that the only defensible principle of ethics and social policy is pleasure, and that pleasure could be determined only by each individual for himself or herself. Public policy should not, from Bentham's perspective, attempt to regulate behavior in accordance with religious principle, moral dogma, or custom, but in accordance with the Utilitarian principle, "the greatest good for the greatest number," where "good" is seen as individual pleasure. In addition to a talent for proselytizing (he came up with the term Utilitarianism), James Mill's major contribution to the movement was to convince Bentham that democracy was necessary for the Utilitarian principle to be fulfilled.

Determined to ensure that his eldest child did not share the social prejudices hampering the implementation of rational social policy, James Mill personally supervised John's education. At the age of three, John was learning Greek and arithmetic, and by the age of eight he began algebra and geometry. His father was a severe master, requiring not only that John daily summarize his studies orally but also that he teach his younger siblings. By the time he was old enough to attend a university, there was little point in doing so. Instead, John accepted a position at the East India Company, where his father worked, and remained until the company was abolished after the British government took over the administration of India in 1858.

John Stuart Mill's education was intended to free him from irrational superstitions and sentiments, to make him capable of the sober, disinterested calculation necessary for the application of the Utilitarian principle. Deprived of a childhood, he was in effect born into a philosophical and political movement. The young man became a zealous organizer and effective debater for this movement, and wrote a number of articles in which he argued the Utilitarian case. At the age of twenty-one, however, John suffered a severe bout of depression brought on, he said, by the realization that the achievement of his political goals would not make him happy. Indeed, complete success would leave a void in his life, since it would deprive him of the movement that had hitherto given his life meaning. But when he realized that the movement's success would not give him happiness, even it seemed meaningless.

His depression lingered for months, and he contemplated suicide. Recovery came with the conviction that happiness comes not from pursuing pleasure for itself but as an indirect consequence of pursuing some other aim. Pleasure pursued directly can give only a superficial happiness; striving for meaningful ends is inherently more pleasurable. The idea of *inherent* pleasure contradicted Bentham's insistence that only the individual can determine pleasure. Yet because pleasure remained the criterion by which the consequences of action are evaluated, Mill contended throughout his life that he had not really broken with the Utilitarianism of Bentham and his father.

If there are inherent or higher pleasures, however, those who understand this can claim to know what is best for those who do not. And if the ignorant need guidance, it becomes difficult to argue that democracy is the ideal form of government. Yet this is exactly what John Stuart Mill argued, most notably in *Considerations on Representative Government* and *Utilitarianism*. Indeed, in his most famous essay, *On Liberty*, he maintained that government had no right to protect citizens from their own folly. Although Mill argued that the intellectual elite should try to educate the masses, this could not be accomplished through the use of political authority.

Whatever the validity of his arguments, Mill's later life certainly provided a salutary role model. He became perhaps the leading intellectual of Victorian England and even served for a few years in Parliament. He died in 1873, having achieved fame and influence as a philosopher, economist, and social reformer. He deserves to be considered in many ways the patron saint of modern liberalism.

Human Nature and Rational Motivation

I regard utility as the ultimate appeal on all ethical questions; but it must be utility in the largest sense, grounded on the permanent interests of man as a progressive being.

—*On Liberty*, chap. 1

Bentham's followers refused to postulate a particular conception of human nature because such speculative metaphysical notions led to rigid moral rules and enforced conformity. The ultimate authority on happiness must be the individual; no one can dictate another's pleasurable experiences. Naturally, the pursuit of some pleasures will cause pain for others, and social regulation is necessary. But if happiness is to be maximized, legislation must be guided by the Utilitarian principle, rather than some notion of right and wrong derived from a conception of humanity.

There is, however, a logical problem with Bentham's Utilitarianism. The Utilitarian principle, the greatest good for the greatest number, is not necessarily in everybody's interest. If the application of the principle deprives me (or you) of individual pleasure because my enjoyment of it is incompatible with the pleasure of others, why should I support the principle? Why should people accept the principle whenever they are not among the "greater number" to be served by it? Bentham does not provide any reason for those who can maximize their own pleasure at the expense of others to refrain from doing so. Elaborate and perhaps effective devices might be designed to prevent people from violating the principle, but by what argument can we convince ourselves that we ought to comply with it? Why is the principle a principle? Without a conception of human nature and rational priorities, Bentham could not provide satisfactory answers to these questions.

Mill broke with his father and Bentham on precisely the issue of the existence of rational priorities. Some pleasures were inherently and demonstrably better than others because they give more happiness. Obviously, it is rational for those able to enjoy these higher pleasures to prefer them over lesser pleasures. Mill did not present a catalogue of the higher pleasures, although he explicitly maintained that intellectual pleasures were among the highest. In one of his more famous epigrams, Mill declared that "it is better to be a human being dissatisfied than a pig satisfied; better a Socrates dissatisfied than a fool satisfied."

Socrates most likely would have agreed with this, but certainly the pig and probably the fool would be unimpressed. Irrespective of species, a satiated creature is by definition happy and would have no reason to envy another's inexplicable enjoyment. If I enjoy checkers, what do I care if someone else prefers chess? Why should I believe that chess will give greater pleasure just because it is a more intellectually demanding game? Mill attempted to answer such a question by limiting testimony to those capable of judging both sides of the case; only someone who knows both games can judge their relative worth. Socrates knows what makes fools and pigs happy, and yet could never be satisfied with such crude and shallow pleasures. Neither fools nor pigs, however, are competent judges of the relative worth of pleasures.

As it stands, this is an unconvincing argument. It seems to substitute the issue of intellectual competence for that of individual happiness. A skeptic might even suspect that intellect is as often a handicap as an advantage in the ability to enjoy life. I might have been happier had I never learned to play chess, just as Socrates might have been happier had he lived in blissful ignorance. Yet Mill had a more forceful argument, based not on dubious testimony but on a conception of human nature entailed in his psychology, what he called the "science of character."

Character is the control of one's own emotions and impulses, on which depends the ability to make genuine choices and to be responsible for oneself. Character, then, is a matter of personal competence, and its development is indeed intimately connected with human happiness. To see this, let us grant that Socrates would not necessarily be contemptuous of the things that make pigs happy, and might on occasion enjoy the same pleasures himself. But only a beast can be satisfied forever with beastly pleasures. A human being cannot be completely happy pursuing a specific set of goals, irrespective of their nature, when he or she suspects that there might be superior alternatives. Even though I may grow to hate chess, once aware of this alternative, my enjoyment of checkers would have been impaired until I became competent to compare the two games. For a self-conscious, intelligent creature choosing is essential for happiness, and anything that enhances character, the competence to make choices, enhances the potential for pleasure.

There are, of course, difficult and even painful choices among less than desirable options, and I return to the question of ends in the next section. At this point, it is necessary to consider whether choice is indeed an essential ingredient of human happiness. Many people fear choice and try to avoid responsibility. Is not choice as likely to be as much a source of frustration and anxiety as satisfaction? This objection fails to consider the real nature of satisfaction. Satisfaction is not simply a synonym for pleasure, but is the kind of pleasure experienced with successful effort. It is active, as opposed to passive, pleasure. Challenge and the risk of frustration are not incompatible with satisfaction, but its preconditions. Satisfaction, in the sense of self-satisfaction, comes only with effort to achieve goals and is enhanced both by the importance of the goals being sought and the effort needed to achieve them.

Great pleasure, in other words, requires great aspiration. The pig may be satiated, but cannot know real satisfaction. Those never confronted with great choices, or who limit aspiration in order to avoid the possibility of failure, are deprived of the pleasures of accomplishment. Even the pain of failure is an acceptable cost for the joys of the quest, the satisfaction of being able to play a significant part in meaningful affairs. The enjoyment of chess, for instance, lies in playing the game, rather than in crushing an opponent, which is why experienced players do not seek out and challenge novices. Active pleasures are better than passive pleasures, and the joys of action are more dependent on engagement than victory. This is what Mill learned from the mental crisis of his youth.

Nonetheless, engagement is meaningful only in terms of the goal, and effectiveness is an essential component of happiness. Consequently, anything that increases an individual's ability to make effective choices, such as intellectual analysis, personal discipline, and judiciousness, enlarges the capability for individual pleasure. For human beings, happiness requires choice. It follows that activities requiring skill and creativity are inherently more pleasurable than those that do not.

The Motivational Basis of Social Solidarity

Not only does all strengthening of social ties ... give to each
individual a stronger personal interest in practically consulting

the welfare of others; it also leads him to identify his *feelings* more and more with their good.... He comes... to be conscious of himself as a being who *of course* pays regard to others.
—*Utilitarianism*, chap. 3

There are many activities requiring skill and choice, most either irrelevant or inimical to the happiness of others. If the Utilitarian principle is to be reconciled with Mill's reformulated Utilitarianism, there must be good reason to believe that public service is inherently more pleasurable than either chess or embezzlement. This is especially important for Mill because by his analysis intellectual elites are critical in maintaining social solidarity. But a Utilitarian could expect them to perform this function only if it is pleasurable to do so.

On first consideration, it might seem obvious that social solidarity follows from Utilitarian considerations. It would be exceedingly painful for most people to be hermits. Yet the mere fact of social utility does not lead to social solidarity because the individual is almost never faced with an immediate choice between society or no society. Instead, our choices are among alternative social arrangements. Social dependence creates social interests, but they are as likely to lead to competition and conflict as cooperation and unity. In the short run, at least, the choice among alternative social arrangements typically will be dictated by considerations of personal advantage, rather than the good of society as a whole.

In the long run, however, it is rational to give primacy to common and complementary interests over purely self-regarding ones. Everybody, no matter how selfish, has an interest in the maintenance of social relationships. Class struggle, for example, is inevitable as long as people see their economic interests in class terms. But class war is not likely to enhance anybody's standard of living. The problem is that most individuals do not adopt a long-run perspective. From either ignorance or the usually correct assumption that an individual action, by itself, will not have significant social consequences, short-term considerations of personal gain guide the conduct of most individuals most of the time.

Consequently, social unity will not emerge from the spontaneous interaction of the masses. In one way or another, solidarity requires the intervention of social elites. There are, however, different ways of maintaining social relationships, each of which requires a different kind of elite. One obvious method is to limit self-regarding behavior by repressing it through intimidation and coercion. This requires what might be called *ruling* elites. Another method, requiring what might be called *political* elites, is to manipulate mass sentiments and play on mass fears. From a Utilitarian perspective, each of these methods is bound to be costly, resulting in a good deal of pain. Much preferable is a third method, education, which obviously requires the public engagement of *intellectual* elites.

Education, in this context, aims at increasing awareness of both the diversity of social interests and the social consequences of failing to accommodate these interests to one another. The best way to achieve this goal is for intellectual elites to formulate specific proposals demonstrating how mutually beneficial compromises among conflicting interests might be forged. For instance, it might be possible to demonstrate that labor organization can increase the efficiency of a firm by providing a reliable source of skilled workers, but only if labor union demands do not undermine its ability to compete. Perhaps some form of profit sharing would serve to reconcile these opposing yet interdependent interests, to their mutual benefit.

Whatever the validity of this proposition, the question of immediate relevance is the incentive of intellectual elites to invent such proposals. What explains their concern for social functionality, their willingness to be the disinterested facilitators of social harmony, the fabricators of a common good? From a Utilitarian perspective, the only incentive can be personal happiness, which by Mill's account requires the development and exercise of character. Character concerns the ability to make choices, and if Mill is correct, the higher the level of choice, the greater the character required and the more meaningful the activity. These propositions are all that is needed to establish the inherent advantage of public service over *most* other activities that also engage the intellect.

To illustrate, let us again consider chess and embezzlement. Both require intelligence and inventiveness for success, and embezzlement may entail great risk. Yet neither activity requires the same level of character as public service because neither offers an equivalent breadth of choice. Each is constrained by relatively rigid standards, without which the activity makes no sense. Chess is really no more than a set of rules. Similarly, the embezzler's activity is structured primarily by criminal law, which the miscreant makes no effort to change, only to circumvent. Conversely, while a concern for public affairs certainly must be constrained by considerations of potential consequences, the formulation of public policy cannot be circumscribed by rigid taboos if social problems are to be solved. The formulation of public policy requires that existing rules be evaluated and, if necessary, new rules created.

Other creative activities, the arts, science, and scholarship, might offer equivalent opportunity for choice. Mill's argument does not require that public affairs provide more meaning than all other endeavors, but only that it be sufficiently rewarding to attract many of the intelligent and capable. This it does, even when intellectual elites typically have limited influence on the formulation of public policy. For the Utilitarian principle is not only the most effective basis for achieving social harmony and rational public policy, it also provides those committed to it with meaning and happiness.

The Function and Organization of Authority

The best government is that which is most conducive to Progress. For Progress includes Order, but Order does not include Progress. Progress is a greater degree of that which Order is a less.

—*Considerations on Representative Government*, chap. 2

Although education is the preferred means of achieving solidarity, Mill was not so naive as to believe that informed discussion alone could maintain order or ensure social progress. In fact, most people, even in the most educated and sophisticated of nations, cannot be counted on either to recognize or to give priority to the long-term interests they share with one another. Government is needed to maintain order, to restrain those who would gratify their own pleasure by causing pain to others. Governmental organization is also necessary to administer effectively common interests that cannot be adequately advanced by individual effort, such as postal services, roads, and defense, or perhaps education, sanitation, and welfare.

These two governmental functions stem from individual limitations, either of character or expertise. The most important function of government, however, is neither protection nor technical proficiency, but the development of character within citizens. Governments, according to Mill, must encourage progress, rather than simply maintain order. Put in terms of utility, the purpose of government cannot just be to facilitate the greatest pleasure for the greatest number, but also to maximize the *potential* for pleasure by increasing the capacity of citizens to make decisions. In effect, Mill contends that government must work to minimize the defects in character that make government necessary in the first place. Order cannot be achieved without progress.

There are two general reasons for the necessity of this kind of progress. The first derives from the consequences of failing to develop a relatively high level of competence among citizens. A regime might be able to maintain order in the short run by following a policy of keeping its population docile through impoverishment and ignorance. In the long run, however, such a policy will lead to disaster. For governments exist in competitive environments, and maintaining control of their own populations cannot be their chief end. To compete economically requires a skilled and energetic labor force, just as military might requires disciplined, motivated troops. A nation of slaves is doomed in a free world.

Even with the absence of external pressure, such a policy will lead to social decline and political disorder. The first reason for the necessity of progress concerns the ability of citizens to do what is necessary to maintain their regime, the second concerns their willingness to do it. As previously discussed, all things being equal it is rational for individuals to give priority to the interests they share with others over purely self-regarding interests. Yet to make this choice consistently they must see their own interests as interconnected with those of society at large. They must be able to take a long-term, rather than a short-term, perspective on social affairs. But if citizens are excluded from public affairs, they will develop neither the ability to deal with public policy nor the willingness to consider the potential consequences of their decisions for society. Instead, they will pursue a narrow version of their interests, competing with one another and attempting to evade social obligations imposed by political authority.

These three governmental functions—protection of individuals, management of common interests, and, especially, education for public life—can best be achieved by a well-designed representative government. Yet Mill's reasons for advocating representative democracy differ significantly from his father's. Both were concerned with providing a mechanism for articulating individual interests, but the younger Mill did not look on representation simply as a device for correctly calculating the greatest benefit for the greatest number. Instead, the primary purpose of representative institutions is to encourage individuals to broaden their notion of personal interests. In other words, a well-functioning representative democracy serves to educate citizens as to their true interests more than it helps them get what they initially want.

This educational function is likely to be served only if those engaged in public life are forced to talk to one another, and this can be assured only if no single interest has a monopoly of power. Consequently, representative democracy will not serve Mill's purpose very well if a majority is too easily formed. Debate is likely to last just as long as it takes to form a majority coalition, for an all-powerful majority has no need to listen to a powerless minority. For this reason, Mill advocated a system of "proportional representation," where the number of representatives a party gains is determined by the proportion of the total popular vote it receives, rather than the number of separate districts it wins. This means that very small parties, even if unable to win in any single district, can win some legislative seats. It also drastically reduces the probability that a single party could win a majority of seats.

As parties cannot win a majority outside the legislature, they have to try to work one out within the legislature, through debate. Proportional representation, then, assures that almost all interests are heard and forces their advocates to talk to one another. Equally important, each legislative faction will want the most articulate and persuasive advocates in the legislature and will, therefore, be inclined to recruit legislative candidates from among intellectual elites. So here we have it: Public involvement is encouraged through open electoral politics, a prominent role is given to people of intellect, and public debate expands social consciousness.

None of this will work, however, if the legislature has too much control over policy proposals. According to Mill, policy initiatives ought to come from the executive branch of government, rather than from legislators themselves. The legislature's functions are to question, to debate, and to approve or disapprove, but not to govern. Government is much more a matter of practicality and expertise than of will and desire. Let the administrative experts determine what is feasible, and the legislative representatives what is acceptable.

There is a still more important reason for limiting the power of the legislature. If public consciousness is to be heightened and individuals of intellect sought as political advocates, debate must be the primary method of creating a majority. But if the legislature has the power to propose and revise legislation, compromise among the more powerful interests will be as likely to determine policy disputes as debate among all parties. In other words, mutual accommodation of some existing interests at the expense of others will supplant the collective search for common interests. To minimize the backdoor trading in special favors and maximize public debate, the legislature must be required to focus its attention on the advisability of a proposal as a whole, rather than on those parts that affect one interest or another.

Mill's General Theory of Political Change and Stability

The natural tendency of representative government, as of modern civilization, is toward collective mediocrity.... But though the superior intellects and characters will necessarily be outnumbered, it makes a great difference whether or not they are heard.
—*Considerations on Representative Government*, chap. 7

Whatever inhibits the development of character and civic consciousness contributes to social inefficiency and eventually leads to political instability. Authoritarian governments, defined as those that discourage political participation, are inherently inefficient and the most prominent source of political instability. They are socially inefficient because they stifle talent, energy, and self-reliance, and they are politically unstable because they induce shortsighted opportunism.

Opportunism is fostered by restricting opportunities for social choice. When people cannot involve themselves with questions of public policy, they will naturally turn their attention elsewhere, which means they will become chiefly concerned with protecting the immediate interests of themselves and their families, trusting that some combination of the ruling elite, chance, and God will take care of the rest. No sense of social responsibility will restrain competition among organized interests. The government will have to control this competition, which it will do by playing interests off against one another, or by purchasing the support of one interest by repressing competitors.

New interests are especially likely to be repressed, out of fear that new contenders either will upset the balance of interests or will threaten an interest favored by the ruling elite. Consequently, such governments are slow to accept social or technological improvements that might give rise to additional organized interests. Unable to trust their own people, authoritarian governments, like authoritarian individuals, fear novelty. Obsolescence, and therefore inefficiency, becomes policy.

In the long run, it is disastrous policy. Juggling is a short-term activity, and the logic of interest conflict leads inexorably to social polarization. If a society is not divided between the haves and the have-nots, it will be split into the satisfied and the dissatisfied. Sooner or later, diverse interests will array themselves into two coalitions. In the absence of common commitment to shared interests, something akin to civil war is a constant threat. A ruling elite might attempt to appeal to traditional values or ideological ideals. But given the low level of civic consciousness caused by a restrictive political system, such efforts are likely to be futile. Sooner or later, authoritarian regimes must rely on coercion, and for this reason they are inherently unstable.

Although authoritarianism is the most prominent source of political instability, it is not the most dangerous. Indeed, as industrialization and the advance of technology require higher levels of education and an ever greater diversity of interdependent interests, authoritarian rule can be expected to be displaced by representative democracy. Faced with the complex demands of modern society, the chronic instability of authoritarianism will eventually lead to the elimination of its source. Since the problems of authoritarian rule are becoming increasing irrelevant, the most dangerous source of instability in the modern world is the tendency within modern representative democracies also to suppress diversity and resist novelty.

To some extent these potential defects of representative democracy are the result of its strengths. As previously discussed, the advantages of representative institutions are derived from the debate they foster. Debate not only encourages the development of individual character but also increases civic consciousness by enlisting citizens in a search for common interests. Because our interests are interdependent, this process results in an ever-growing body of programs and policy that are no longer controversial. Debate increasingly is focused on the loose ends and details of a much larger consensus simply taken for granted by almost all participants. But as the stakes become progressively lower, political debate becomes more marginal and attracts less attention, especially since those advocating major change are likely to be seen as extremists with minuscule political prospects.

Whatever positive influence political debate might have on the development of character is bound to be diminished as politics itself is considered of dubious importance. Much worse, however, is the tendency in modern societies for the populace to become intolerant of diverse beliefs and lifestyles. Mass democracy encourages a conformity of opinion and behavior that can be more oppressive than the political domination of a ruling elite. I am speaking, of course, of the "tyranny of public opinion." Once a large portion of the population enjoys a degree of comfort and security, there will be little recognition of the value of alternatives. Diversity is more likely to be seen as a threat than an advantage. And once the people have been recognized as the source of governmental legitimacy, the people will tend to think itself justified in persecuting those refusing to conform to conventional ideas and practices.

This intolerance of diversity creates an environment hostile to debate, which has two detrimental consequences. The first is simply stagnation. Without a forum to consider alternatives seriously, either in the legislature or the media, the possibilities for reform and improvement are much diminished. A stagnant society can maintain itself as long as it is in equilibrium with its environment, but in the long run all history demonstrates that even the most successful civilizations must adapt in order to survive.

The second consequence is more serious. Without the challenge of debate, society will decline even in the absence of externally induced crises. As political debate becomes constrained by consensus, attention will turn from civic to personal affairs, and representative democracy begins to suffer the same effects of the decline of civic consciousness endemic to authoritarianism. Once again, competition among organized interests will be unrestrained by a sense of social responsibility. Initially, of course, the consensus on policies maximizing mutual interests will confine conflict to petty disputes over minor advantages. But if the process continues unchecked, it will undermine the consensus itself because it will create people unable to appreciate and use the accomplishments of the past.

Character is required to make choices, but choices are required to develop character. An individual never confronted with meaningful and challenging alternatives will never reach a high level of competence. But if all portentous issues had been resolved and all major questions answered, would people need to be competent? They would. Otherwise, they would neither understand nor be concerned with the answers. The answers would become mere formulas, said when things like that are supposed to be said. Like a religious creed that has become staid and conventional, all affirm but few feel. These few are the only ones likely really to understand the creed, and they will be the only ones for whom it will actually make a difference in their daily choices.

So, too, with the accumulated political wisdom produced by success in meeting past challenges. While almost all political participants may affirm the policies that have come to be accepted as in the common interest, their immediate concerns are likely to be the special interests of the groups for which they are the agents. As a consequence, the political consensus tends to be reduced to a set of rhetorical formulas, useful for garnering support rather than guiding action.

By itself, rhetoric never stopped anybody ambitious from doing anything they really wanted to do. If a policy consensus is to be saved from being undermined piecemeal, political participants sufficiently powerful to be heard must defend it. This requires not only political activists more concerned with the public welfare than special interests, but also debate on how best to maximize this goal. In other words, for a policy consensus to remain effective and be adapted to new circumstances, dissidents are essential to keep the debate alive.

Some of Mill's institutional prescriptions for ensuring debate among individuals committed to public service have already been discussed. They include proportional representation and a stringent separation of executive and legislative functions. Proportional representation assures both that minorities have the opportunity to be heard and that all parties will have an incentive to recruit representatives from intellectual elites. In this context, a strict separation of executive and legislative functions serves to focus legislative debate on the implications of policy proposals for common, rather than special, interests. Yet Mill did not presume that institutional prescriptions alone would be sufficient in modern mass societies to preserve a level of debate adequate for continual social progress. Not only must intellectually gifted individuals engage in open debate over what best serves common interests, they must also recognize the limits of what can be accomplished by public authority.

One of these limits is defined by the "harm principle," which stipulates that government must never coerce individuals for their own good, but only for the protection of others. As long as behavior or opinions hurt no one but those who hold them, they should be discussed, but not repressed. Adherence to the harm principle encourages the continual creation of alternatives, essential for keeping debate alive and for adapting to new circumstances. Willingness to suppress alternatives is tantamount to believing that we are so certain in our opinions that we need not prove their superiority in debate. If we are to have debate, we cannot decide beforehand which alternatives we will tolerate. Moreover, character, the chief end of good government, cannot be developed through coercion. Individuals must arrive at their own conclusions and make their own choices.

Just as individual character requires personal freedom, so too does social progress require democracy. And just as personal freedom requires tolerance, so too does democracy. Publicly engaged intellectuals must, on the one hand, acknowledge the limitations imposed by the harm principle, but on the other, they must be willing to see this principle violated by popular majorities. Mill even acknowledged that youth must be made to conform to conventional prejudices if the public is to feel sufficiently secure to tolerate unconventional adult behavior. In other words, to have any effect the harm principle itself must be limited. Popular rule is often unjust, but it is always legitimate. When public debate fails to educate the public, the only recourse is more debate.

The Politics of Character

Because the challenge of a meaningful task affords the highest form of happiness, public service is bound to be a fulfilling endeavor. Yet it is always frustrating to be a reformer. Popular prejudices resist the force of reason, and unprincipled political hacks have a vested interest in rhetorically reinforcing such prejudices in order to enhance their own power. Ignorance and unscrupulous ambition are the formidable opponents that inevitably confront a progressive politics.

The greatest impediment to progress, however, is not the threat of these open opponents, but its own success. With success come victories to protect. Indeed, successful reformers typically acquire public office to ensure that the policies they have championed are properly implemented and administered. Even if one resists the complacent self-satisfaction that often accompanies high office and success, it is natural to treasure the fruits of past victories. Today's reformers may become tomorrow's reactionaries, all the more dangerous to reform because they will unwittingly have metamorphosized into traditionalists, too preoccupied with past accomplishments to realize that they are the obstacles, rather than the agents, of progress.

A Brief Guide to the Literature

The most complete biography of Mill is Michael St. John Packe's *The Life of John Stuart Mill* (1954). Of the alternatives, among the most interesting is Bruce Mazlish's psychoanalytical study of Mill and his father,

James and John Stuart Mill: Father and Son in the Nineteenth Century (1975). On the development of the Utilitarian movement before John Stuart Mill, in both its theoretical and political dimensions, refer to Elie Halevy, *The Growth of Philosophic Radicalism* (1928). For a detailed study of Mill's involvement with the movement, see Joseph Hamburger, *Intellectuals in Politics: John Stuart Mill and the Philosophic Radicals* (1965). Two useful surveys of Mill's thought as a whole, both emphasizing philosophical issues rather than social theory, are Karl Britton, *John Stuart Mill: Life and Philosophy* (1969), and Alan Ryan, *The Philosophy of John Stuart Mill* (1970). Ryan's intent is to demonstrate the unity of Mill's thought by showing how his analysis of the possibility of a science of society informed his discussion of ethics and social affairs.

Yet the possibility of a science of society, at least as apparently conceived by Mill, entails the possibility of experts and raises questions about the relationship between expertise and authority. Concerning social knowledge, Mill is definitely an elitist, and some scholars have questioned Mill's democratic credentials. Most notably, Maurice Cowling, in *Mill and Liberalism* (1963), argues that Mill was actually an authoritarian and his political thought an attempt to enhance the influence of a certain kind of intellectual elite while diminishing that of traditional elites. For a critical response to this thesis, as well as to a number of other negative assessments of Mill's work, see John C. Rees's posthumously published book, *John Stuart Mill's* On Liberty (1985).

One of the scholars criticized by Rees is Gertrude Himmelfarb, who maintains, in *On Liberty and Liberalism: The Case of John Stuart Mill* (1974), that there are two irreconcilable Mills, the libertine who wrote *On Liberty* and the prudent moralist of most of his other works. The existence of somewhat less spectacular inconsistencies in Mill's arguments has been asserted by many commentators. One of the more engaging is Robert Paul Wolff, *The Poverty of Liberalism* (1968). Two works focusing on Mill's political theory and claiming, in varying degree, to find consistency are John M. Robson, *The Improvement of Mankind: The Social and Political Thought of John Stuart Mill* (1968), and Dennis F. Thompson, *John Stuart Mill and Representative Government* (1976). Thompson's book is notable in that he makes a conscious attempt to relate Mill's thought to contemporary studies of democracy within political science.

Marx and the
Politics of History

The Historical Marx

Karl Marx was a true cosmopolitan. He came of age in Germany, formulated the first outline of his social theory in France and Belgium, and lived the last half of his life in England. He was neither very concerned with nor unduly influenced by political developments in any particular country. By his analysis, the only political activity that might have an appreciable impact on human history is that which aims at the transformation of society itself, which results in social revolution rather than a mere change in regime. Meaningful politics should not aim at acquiring governmental power but at creating the kind of society where neither government nor politics itself could serve any useful purpose.

Born in Trier, then part of Prussia, in 1818, Marx was the eldest son of a well-educated and moderately successful lawyer. His father was an assimilated Jew, who converted to Protestantism in order to avoid the effects of anti-Jewish laws, which would have prohibited the practice of his profession. The conversion was facilitated by the fact that the senior Marx was a child of the Enlightenment. He had long since abandoned the religious practices of his ancestors. Yet he was a liberal living under a conservative and repressive regime, forced to deny his ancestry and to refrain from expressing opinions on social and political matters. He must have borne the costs of personal compromise daily. At least this can be inferred from his son's refusal ever to bear such costs, always preferring to risk the consequences of expressing his beliefs.

After a year as a law student at a provincial university, Marx was sent to the university at Berlin in the hope that exposure to the intellectual center of the German-speaking world would lead him to take his studies more seriously. During his second year at Berlin, his father died. Marx gave up the study of law, becoming instead a student of philosophy. Philosophy in Berlin was completely dominated by the thought of Hegel, who argued that history was unified by the development of rational self-consciousness. Indeed, with Hegel's philosophy, through which the apparent irrationalities of the past appear as necessary steps in the development of a world where everything has its rational place and function, history is at an end. Things happen, of course, but only have meaning insofar as they contribute to the maintenance of civilization and culture as it is given.

What fascinated Marx in this extremely conservative view of the world was the notion of rationality in history; what repelled him was the idea that such rationality has been largely realized in the present. Instead of believing, with Hegel, that the "real is rational," Marx joined a loose association of young intellectuals, called the Young Hegelians, in attempting to establish that the "rational is real." Put differently, they attempted to find in the rationality of history a basis for criticizing and overcoming the irrationalities of the present.

After leaving the university, Marx edited a liberal paper critical of feudal injustices and oppressive governmental policy. Eventually the paper was banned by the reactionary Prussian government. Having no other prospect of employment, he agreed to become co-editor of a radical journal in Paris. There Marx became a socialist, meeting the leading radical theorists of the time, as well as his lifelong collaborator, Friedrich Engels. With Engels's help, he formulated the basic outline of his theoretical system, a relatively complete version of which first appears in the initial pages of a work unpublished in his lifetime, *The German Ideology*. Two years later, in 1848, he and Engels succinctly sketched these ideas in the famous polemical tract, *The Communist Manifesto*.

Even before the wave of revolutions that swept Europe in 1848, Marx had been deported from France to Belgium. After the publication of the *Manifesto*, the Belgian authorities deported him back to France. With the initial success of the revolution in Prussia, Marx returned to Germany to edit yet another radical paper. With the collapse of the revolution and the return of a reactionary regime, he was once again deported, this time to England. There he remained until his death, in 1883. During these long years of exile, he and his family often experienced extreme poverty. Nonetheless, they were years of great accomplishment. He completed the first volume of *Das Kapital*, his painstaking critique of the dynamics of capitalism. This work eventually made him famous, and by the time of his death he was recognized throughout Europe as the leading theoretician of socialism.

Human Nature and Rational Motivation

The object of labor is ... the *objectification of man's species life;* for he duplicates himself not only ... intellectually, but also actively, in reality, and therefore he contemplates himself in a world that he has created.

—*Economic and Philosophic Manuscripts of 1848*

To be human is to be free. Human freedom, however, means more than mere lack of constraint. Flags may be "free" to flap in the wind, but it makes little sense to suggest that persons are free when their willful activity is either aimless or futile. Human freedom requires power and knowledge. We cannot be free unless we know what we want and how to achieve it, unless our power serves our purposes. To say the same thing from another perspective, a free choice not only must be voluntary, it must also be informed. For choice must be rational to be genuine. Anyone incapable of seeing that $2 \times 2 = 4$ is simply incapable of freedom.

Constraints limit freedom only if irrational and arbitrary; rational constraints cannot be considered incompatible with human freedom. For this reason, Hegel maintained that true freedom is possible only if the world is rational. After all, no one doubts that most human experience is constrained by one's natural and social environment. Only by affirming the rationality of human history, indeed of the universe, can humans be free. For most people, at least in the West, religion has given freedom through faith in God's will. Although mere mortals cannot completely understand His plan for the world, the faithful cannot doubt its ultimate rationality. For everything has been created for a purpose. The intent of Hegel's philosophy is to provide the same sense of freedom for those unable to have faith in the existence of a personal divinity.

He attempted to do this by demonstrating that we live in a rational world that came to be by a rational process. Indeed, the world is itself a manifestation of universal reason, and all forms of understanding, such as science, philosophy, and religion, are forms of self-consciousness; that is, reason conscious of itself. In the last analysis, consciousness is cultural, just as thinking, dependent on language, is social. Morality and duty simply express the behavioral code rationally appropriate to our particular role in the rational whole. Individual freedom is attained by understanding the rational necessity of our social and cultural life and attending to our social duties.

Marx accepted Hegel's identification of human freedom with rationality, and even its social nature, but he rejected the idea that we must accept the world as rational in order to be free. Freedom depends on our *making* the world rational, rather than on simply assuming on faith that it is so and interpreting it accordingly. In this sense, Marx is a "materialist," as opposed to an "idealist." And how do we make the world rational? We do so through work, through our ability to domesticate nature and turn it to our purposes. And what are our purposes, what guides our struggle with nature? At the most basic level, our primary goal must be survival. We have to subdue nature in order to produce the goods on which our survival depends.

It is not, however, the survival of the individual that guides our confrontation with the world. Marx is not an individualist, at least not in the same sense as Hobbes or Locke. Individuals only think of themselves when they must, for both the means and the meaning of individual existence are embedded in social life. Unless deluded by peculiar social doctrines, we readily recognize that our technical ability to cope with nature is the product of social learning. Moreover, as isolated individuals, we would have little for which to live. Almost all work, indeed almost all human endeavor is to a significant extent collective in both its conduct and its goals. Humans are, to use Marx's phrase, "species beings." As conscious creatures, we know that we are not mere individuals. It is, therefore, natural for people in extreme circumstances to sacrifice themselves for the good of their fellows just because they do not necessarily see it as a sacrifice.

Social survival provides the goal, but freedom provides the incentive. For an individual, mastering nature through work is its own reward. In confronting the problems of production humans realize their potential to control reality and develop their natural capacities. They learn by doing, rather than by memorizing, and they can confirm what they know by using their knowledge, rather than having it certified by authority. They develop their reason and simultaneously create a more rational world, one ordered according to human needs. Failures are inevitable, and environmental constraints will never be completely overcome. Nevertheless, it is the effort that defines us as human, not success. We make ourselves free through work.

The Motivational Basis of Social Solidarity

The social power ... which arises through the co-operation of different individuals as it is determined by the division of labor, appears to these individuals, since their co-operation is not voluntary ..., as an alien force existing outside them ..., which they cannot control.

—*The German Ideology*

"Labor makes free" was the inscription the Nazis placed above the gates to the infamous concentration camp at Auschwitz. It was an obvious lie in that context. Yet labor typically is perceived to be burdensome rather than liberating, and Marx believed this perception to be largely correct. Much of his thought can be seen as an attempt to explain how liberating work is transformed into oppressive labor. In brief, the transformation takes place when work is controlled by someone other than the laborer. When this happens, work becomes alienated in the sense that it no longer serves to enhance the laborer's freedom. To the contrary, when workers no longer control their own labor, they are rendered dependent and ineffectual. In fact, their dependence and inability to change their environment become the mainstays of social solidarity.

Free individuals, for reasons previously discussed, will naturally cooperate in the pursuit of collective ends. Social solidarity is a problem only in societies where work becomes alienated, and individuals are forced to consider personal advantage before any common good. This is self-evident in a slave society, where the exploitation of labor rests on the naked power of masters. More interesting, and certainly more relevant, are cases in which a class dominates primarily through the acquiescence of the exploited, rather than by force. By Marx's analysis, this is the kind of society in which we live.

The distinguishing characteristic of modern societies is a general division of labor. Primitive societies have only a rudimentary division of labor, usually based on age and gender. Technological development, however, is accompanied by occupational specialization, which inevitably results in a class society. Take, for example, a hypothetical agricultural society at a relatively modest stage of technological development, roughly corresponding to that of medieval Europe. A diversity of occupations would exist even in this relatively simple society, but three main classes would subsume most of them. The largest class would be peasants, those working the land and caring for animals. Artisans, such as metalworkers, would constitute a much smaller class, manufacturing the more elaborate agricultural tools and other products not easily made in the household. Finally, there must be a controlling class, to plan, keep records, and coordinate the activities of all.

Accounts must be kept and activities coordinated because each group of workers depends for its livelihood on the rest. The advantages of specialization come only with mutual dependence. The more elaborate the division of labor, the greater the interdependence and the more coordination is needed for effective production. This interdependence has both positive and negative implications for social solidarity. On the positive side, of course, interdependence forces cooperation and encourages the identification of individual and common interests. The negative implications, however, are severe. Production may be collective, but consumption is always individual. Goods produced have to be distributed, inevitably leading to competition among the classes created by the division of labor.

If each class were given an opportunity to present its case, each would emphasize the importance of its contribution to production. Peasants would call attention to the extent of their toil, artisans would argue that a single skilled craftsman contributes more to production than several field hands, and controllers would accentuate the importance of coordination, pointing out that competition itself must be managed. But such arguments rarely take place and cannot influence actual patterns of distribution in any case. By Marx's analysis, the controlling class always prevails, irrespective of its actual economic importance.

The class controlling the primary means of production is everywhere the ruling class. In our hypothetical agricultural society the primary means of production is land. Those who determine what will be grown or raised on the land and how it will be done also determine who and how many will participate, as well as the nature of their participation. Once this power is legally institutionalized into property relations, the lords of the soil have no need to listen to the claims of other classes or even to argue their own. Indeed, distribution is determined largely by the worth of property involved in production, and those who possess only their own labor will fare little better than slaves who own nothing at all.

Although the ruling class has little need to listen or argue, it does need to educate. Class conflict is an ever-present possibility because class tension is inherent in the division of labor. Social solidarity can be assured only if class conflict is seen by all classes as both destructive and morally wrong. The educated and more intelligent members of society, irrespective of class, need little convincing of the destructive consequences of class conflict. Anything that disrupts production obviously undermines the well-being of all. If alternative ways of producing essential goods were known, each class might try to impose a method enhancing its members' interests. Typically, however, there is only one "state of the art" technology, compared to which all others are obsolete and inefficient. In our hypothetical agricultural society, for example, only the desperate or the stupid would want to be nomadic hunter-gatherers.

Yet the technical efficiency of prevailing arrangements does not ensure the voluntary acquiescence of the lower classes to the privileges and power of the ruling class. The unequal distribution of advantages and opportunities in class society almost guarantees that there will be many desperate and ignorant people. If social solidarity is to be maintained, these people must feel that they are morally obliged to accept their station in life. The ruling elite must not only explain how the system provides for material needs but must also plausibly claim that it serves the highest human ideals.

Whatever the nature of these ideals, they are no more than palliatives. Humans invent religious, nationalistic, or racial ideals to compensate for their lack of control over their environment and themselves. Religion and ideology are the products of alienation. By making workers mutually dependent and forcing them to use their labor at the behest of others, the division of labor destroys any possibility for true freedom. Deprived of the ability to master their environment through their own efforts, individuals are prone to identify with mental fictions such as gods or nations. These supernatural entities enjoy all the power and control denied to their worshipers, and for this reason provide a vicarious experience of freedom, substituting for the real thing.

Religion, in Marx's words, is the "opium of the people," and philosophies such as Hegel's serve the same purpose for intellectuals. They are forms of "false consciousness." Imaginary ideals provide meaning to those unable to find fulfillment in the real world. In the process, people are able to accommodate themselves to an oppressive, stultifying existence. This by itself reduces the threat that class tension will lead to class conflict. Typically, this effect is reinforced by substantive beliefs serving to rationalize social conditions and encourage acceptance of social duties. Religions, for instance, often explain suffering in this world as a condition for finding redemption and compensation in the next, encouraging an ethic of patient acceptance.

The Function and Organization of Authority

> When in the course of development, class distinctions have disappeared ... the public power will lose its political character. Political power, properly so called, is merely the organized power of one class for oppressing another.
>
> —*Manifesto of the Communist Party*

Despite his commitment to human liberation and equality, Marx was not a democrat. In fact, he had little to say about the relative advantages of one form of government over another because he did not think it made any significant difference. Nor did he think that it made much difference who was in power at any particular time. All governments are repressive. All governments, irrespective of ideological orientation or the degree of opposition they tolerate, serve the interests of the ruling class. Indeed, they do so even when power is exercised by leaders or political parties genuinely hostile to economic elites.

Government is necessarily a tool of the ruling class because its chief function is to maintain order. Although modern governments provide crucial services in such important policy domains as education, sanitation, and transportation, any kind of effective public policy requires public peace. Consequently, the police function of the state is everywhere primary. In maintaining public order, however, the government necessarily protects the interests of the ruling class because the basic structure of social organization is imposed by the division of labor. In other words, the order to be preserved is the order in which the ruling class enjoys a strategic advantage over other classes.

Anything disruptive of production is clearly a threat to social order. Since each class exists just because it contributes to production, no government has the prerogative of abolishing one of them. In our hypothetical agricultural society, a peasant revolt might successfully destroy the authority of landlords. But after burning the fine houses, emptying the wine cellars, and enjoying a short period of respite from toil, some among them will have to take responsibility for seeing that they all go back to work, that artisans are paid for their products, and that sufficient food is stored to make it through the winter. The only question is how long it will take those who assume this responsibility to establish a legal right to control the land, build fine houses, and lay up new stocks of wine.

In class societies, political authority is essential for the same reason social solidarity is a problem. Tension among the classes cannot be eradicated, and when such forms of false consciousness as religion fail to curb class conflict, organized coercion must be available. Whether those who apply the coercion see themselves as agents of the ruling class makes little difference. Indeed, public order may be easier to ensure if the government is controlled by politicians whose power rests on popular support. Even if these popular leaders are genuinely committed to political and economic equality, the practical imperatives of production will force them to restrain popular demands for the redistribution of wealth. The greatest danger of popular government to a ruling class is likely to be higher taxes to pay for social welfare programs; for those who have much to lose, this is a small price to pay for social peace and security. The ruling class does not have to rule to be the ruling class.

Democratic institutions, then, might ameliorate some of the disadvantages suffered by the lower classes, but they can do nothing to alter the fundamental cause of those disadvantages. As long as there is a social division of labor, there will be a ruling class. In reality, the myth of popular sovereignty, like religion, is no more than a form of false consciousness that serves to placate the disadvantaged, especially when combined with nationalism, which is almost always the case. The identification of the individual with such collective fictions as the "nation" or the "people" can bestow a vicarious feeling of drama and power, but this is a pale substitute for genuine freedom. The potential for the real experience of individual freedom through control of one's environment is displaced by the fantasy of "political freedom."

Marx's General Theory of Political Change and Stability

Every new class... achieves its hegemony only on a broader basis than that of the class ruling previously, whereas the opposition of the non-ruling class against the new ruling class later develops all the more sharply and profoundly.

—*The German Ideology*

Even though Marx owes his fame largely to his analysis and critique of capitalist society, to this point I have refrained from referring to capitalism. Instead, I have attempted to illustrate his conceptual assumptions through reference to a simple, hypothetical agrarian society. This is because I am chiefly concerned with elucidating Marx's general conceptual assumptions, rather than any particular application of them. Moreover, it is Marx the political theorist who is of interest here, not Marx the economist.

Nevertheless, one cannot maintain a sharp distinction between political theory and economic analysis if one is to understand Marx's theory of political change. For according to his analysis, significant political change is possible only when preceded by change in the "mode of production." The mode of production refers primarily to the dominant technology and the social division of labor it requires, and secondarily to the economic arrangements by which the ruling class is able to appropriate "surplus" production. One use of this surplus, of course, is to enhance the standard of living of the ruling class. Another is reinvestment, such as the replacement of worn-out equipment or the improvement of roads, harbors, storage facilities, and so forth. Yet the most essential use of economic surplus is to support the complex of social arrangements, including political institutions, that Marx called the "superstructure" of society.

In addition to government, the superstructure encompasses religious, educational, and family organization; the artistic expression of the lifestyles imposed by such social structures; and the theological, philosophical, or ideological ideas justifying them. In short, the superstructure represents the behavioral and mental adaptations to the necessities of economic production. For this reason, significant change in superstructural institutions occurs only after prior change in a society's mode of production. Yet the superstructure cannot be dismissed as superfluous. For production requires individual incentive and discipline. Consequently, a viable mode of production must incorporate a means of extracting sufficient surplus to support the institutional arrangements and cultural sentiments that enable humans to cope with one another and accommodate themselves to their fate.

Nor can the mode of production be considered the "cause" of the superstructure. Ideas and practices incompatible with economic necessities cannot prevail, but this does not imply that there can be only one way to adapt to these necessities. Economic necessity only restricts the range of viable options; it does not determine our choices. Only in a limited sense, then, is Marx a social determinist. Despite an occasional extravagant prediction, especially regarding the inevitability of communism, there are only two inevitabilities in Marx's thought. The first is the inevitability of change in the superstructure once the mode of production has evolved, and the other is the inevitable collapse of capitalism.

The rise of capitalism, however, was not inevitable. Capitalism was a coincidental result of the decline of the feudal system of medieval Europe, which was itself the result of historical contingencies. The complex contingencies surrounding the rise and decline of European feudalism are controversial, and the viability of Marx's social theory does not rest on his treatment of them. Consequently, I illustrate the logic of Marx's analysis of historical change by outlining how our hypothetical agrarian society might have evolved into a capitalist system.

In such a society both production and consumption are local. There is little trade, so there is little need for money. Artisans are typically paid in kind, and peasants fulfill their obligations to the lords of the land with a significant portion of the harvest. Landlord control of storage facilities, and therefore of distribution, is likely to be the primary means of appropriating surplus production. In this decentralized system much of this surplus will have to be devoted to military resources, which is likely to be a preoccupation of ruling-class males. Given that there is need for neither widespread literacy nor a class of practically oriented technicians and administrators, much of the surplus will support the propagation of some form of otherworldly religion. When all goes well, religion will be a chief preoccupation of almost everybody, especially the peasants.

If left to itself, this system could continue indefinitely. Change will be stimulated by external influences, rather than internal development. New opportunities for travel to exotic civilizations, for example, are likely to make possible a lucrative trade in luxury goods. Such items typically are easily portable and appeal to the only people in the system who have the cash to make a market, the ruling class. Trade requires merchants, who until these developments would have been a marginal and somewhat disreputable group. For in the simple agricultural society, where exchange consists largely of barter among producers, merchants are generally not needed, and their status as "middlemen" would make them generally despised.

Now they become the nucleus of a class, and their increasing importance in producing the goods necessary for social life inevitably alters social organization. First, they need things to trade. This results in industry and factories. Industry, in turn, requires workers. With opportunities for factory work, peasants are freed of obligations tying them to the land. Workers cannot be paid in kind because they are producing for a market, and so currency is required. Now a greater percentage of the population has money, and markets for everyday necessities, in addition to luxury goods, are created. This leads to growth in the number of merchants and factory owners, who constitute an emerging class, which Marx called the "bourgeoisie."

Money does more than promote the growth of markets and free peasants from obligations to the lords of the land; more fundamentally, it makes possible the accumulation of savings and greatly facilitates investment in future production. In short, the existence of a money economy is necessary for the existence of a "capitalist" economy. In the broadest sense, capital is simply deferred consumption, and to some degree is required by all economic systems. A capitalist economy, however, depends on regular investment of savings to create new productive opportunities. Consider the investment required several centuries ago to send a ship to sea with a cargo to trade for goods at an exotic port. The ship and its equipment had to be purchased, the cargo and provisions for the crew supplied. Then the investors had to wait two or three years for their ship to return (if it did) in order to recoup their investment.

This is risky business. It requires huge amounts of capital, which in turn can be created only by huge profits. We need not worry about how such capital might have been initially accumulated. The important point is that capital, rather than land, becomes the primary means of production and that the difference between cost and selling price, rather than control of storage facilities or direct confiscation, becomes the mechanism by which surplus production is appropriated by the new ruling class. The mode of production has been changed, and we have capitalism.

Unlike the relatively static economy of the simple agricultural system, capitalism necessarily leads to continuous growth of productive capacity. Competition among capitalists for a share of the market compels investors to attempt to sell at a lower price than competitors through greater productive efficiency. More fundamentally, investors will seek to create new markets, usually by inventing new commodities, leading to an explosion of technological innovation and material goods. For all his criticisms of capitalism, Marx insisted that this system of continual investment would create a productive capacity potentially sufficient for the elimination of material scarcity.

Yet capitalism is doomed. For this mode of production contains an internal contradiction. On the one hand, ever-increasing amounts of capital must be invested. On the other, the means by which capital is accumulated systematically destroys the markets for the goods it so successfully produces. The source of capital investment is, of course, surplus production. The means by which the bourgeoisie appropriates this surplus is through profit, the difference between the cost of production and the selling price of commodities. In the last analysis, the cost of production is determined primarily by the cost of labor. Since competition prohibits raising prices, the only way profits usually can be increased is to reduce labor costs. To reduce the return to labor, however, means diminished purchasing power, which means smaller markets.

The result is periodic economic depressions brought on by overproduction; the system produces more goods than people can purchase. Smaller, less competitive companies suffer bankruptcy during these economic downturns. As a consequence, the bourgeois class shrinks, while the working class, the "proletariat," expands. A greater supply of workers makes it easier to lower wages. This results in an ever-decreasing standard of living and depressions of greater frequency and severity. There is poverty amid plenty. The system cannot go on indefinitely. If it is not overthrown, it will simply collapse into chaos.

Normally, a ruling class cannot be dislodged. Its status is derived from the division of labor; whoever performs its function will control the means of production and determine the distribution of goods. Once its function is no longer essential, however, a ruling class is vulnerable to those who play a more important role in the production of wealth. The peasants could never free themselves from the lords of the land, but the bourgeoisie could displace these landlords because control of the land is of little importance in a capitalist system. If an obsolete ruling class clings to its privileged position through its control of the institutions of the superstructure, its rule increasingly will be viewed as a costly, unjustified burden. If it refuses to yield, eventually there will be a revolution. Old institutions and ways of thinking will be smashed, and new ones, more appropriate for the support of the new economic order, will be established.

By Marx's analysis, the bourgeoisie is making itself economically irrelevant. In the later stages of capitalism, the capitalists are producing for a nonexistent market. Even more important, the level of material abundance made possible by compulsive investment diminishes the need for further investment. As these irrationalities of the system become apparent, all the cultural resources of the superstructure cannot obscure them from an increasingly impoverished, growing proletariat.

As the irrelevance of the bourgeoisie becomes obvious, the proletariat not only has the opportunity to displace the bourgeoisie but to abolish class society itself.

Social classes are mandated by the division of labor, but the division of labor is necessary only as long as production requires social regimentation. Technological progress, a consequence of forced investment, eventually eliminates the need to compel sections of the population to do certain kinds of work. A sufficiently high level of technology will permit people to labor at the tasks they find meaningful and necessary. A second consequence of forced investment, abundance, eliminates the need to ration the goods of social production. Together, these consequences of capitalism make *communism* a possibility. Communism is a society based on the principle "from each according to his ability, to each according to his need." Without the necessity of forcing people to work, there will be no owners or bosses. Without scarcity, there will be no markets. Without markets, there will be no money or wages. Without alienation, there will be no churches or nations, and without the threat of class conflict, there will be no state.

Marx had almost nothing to say about how a communist society would work. He was more concerned with giving future generations the opportunity to make it work. For although capitalism is doomed, communism is not really inevitable. The collapse of capitalism will present the proletariat with an opportunity to abolish class society, but the proletariat must be ready to take advantage of this opportunity. First they must see it; they must be "class conscious." Then they must be sufficiently organized to eliminate superstructural institutions, such as private property, that serve primarily to maintain the privileges of an obsolete ruling class. Consequently, it is the task of working-class organizations to organize and educate the proletariat in order to seize power and reorganize society when the opportunity presents itself. In the event of failure, the collapse of capitalism simply will result in regression to a decentralized, technologically more primitive stage of production, and the miserable process of productive expansion will begin again.

History has not yet been kind to Marx's analysis of capitalism's fatal contradictions. The proletariat still waits for its opportunity. Regarding the material standard of living, the wait has not been particularly unpleasant. Workers, often with the assistance of government, seem to have maintained sufficient purchasing power to prevent depressions from becoming more frequent or severe. Their chances of successfully overthrowing the bourgeoisie would appear to be as hopeless as that of the peasants overthrowing the lords of the land in our simple agricultural society. And just as the landlords could have stifled the growth of the bourgeoisie if they had had the foresight to prevent the growth of trade, so too would it seem that the managers of capitalism can protect their markets. But the apparent failure of Marx's analysis of the economic imperatives of capitalism does not necessarily invalidate his political thought. Before we rejoice at capitalism's resilience, we should ask ourselves if most of us have a genuine opportunity to lead fulfilling, meaningful lives. Is our work liberating? Are we free?

The Politics of History

Like government, politics is a necessary consequence of class conflict. Antagonistic social interests created by the division of labor must in some way be reconciled when they cannot be repressed. Although exploited classes might marginally improve their circumstances through political mobilization and negotiation with agents of the ruling class, circumstances cannot be altered fundamentally through political pressure alone. The ruling class rules not primarily because of its political power but because of its control of the means of production. In fact, a ruling class is doomed if it depends primarily on political power to maintain its status. For this would mean that the mode of production has changed, and the control of the means of production has shifted to another class. In other words, ruling classes can be displaced only when they have become economically obsolete. Only then can history be made through politics.

By Marx's analysis, capitalism has reached this stage. Indeed, not only are capitalists economically superfluous, even the division of labor is unnecessary. Politics now can aim higher than the overthrow of the existing ruling class; it can abolish classes altogether. Were it to accomplish this feat, politics itself would be forever unnecessary. It naturally follows that political theory would no longer be needed either to rationalize or to criticize claims of political right.

A Brief Guide to the Literature

Of the many biographies of Marx, Saul K. Padover, *Marx: An Intimate Bi-*

ography (1978), is probably the most readable, even if not the most comprehensive. Isaiah Berlin, *Karl Marx: His Life and Environment* (1948), is more a study of the development of Marx's thought and achieves a certain balance despite the author's lack of sympathy with his subject. Of the many intellectual histories of Marxism, George Lichtheim, *Marxism: An Historical and Critical Study* (1964), is among the most reliable and insightful, but Edmund Wilson, *To the Finland Station* (1940), is the best written. Probably the best survey of Marx's political thought is Shlomo Avineri, *The Social and Political Thought of Karl Marx* (1968). Robert Freedman, *The Marxist System: Economic, Political, and Social Perspectives* (1990), offers a succinct and useful overview of Marx's social and economic thought.

For years, Marx was considered primarily an economic theorist, at least among English-speaking scholars. The discovery and translation of the explicitly philosophical works of his youth precipitated a debate over the existence of an earlier, humanistic Marx and a later, deterministic Marx. Louis Althusser, in *For Marx* (1969), asserts that the latter represents the mature Marx, whereas Robert Tucker, in *Philosophy and Myth in Karl Marx* (1972), claimed that Marx's later analysis of the class struggle in capitalism was simply an external dramatization of the human struggle for self-realization as defined in his philosophical period. Both Istvan Meszaros, in *Marx's Theory of Alienation* (1970), and Bertell Ollman, in *Alienation: Marx's Conception of Man in Capitalist Society* (1971), convincingly argue, each in his own way, that there are no essential incompatibilities between the early and the late Marx.

Marx's theory of capitalist development has often been criticized, most notably by Karl Popper in *The Open Society and Its Enemies* (1957), for being unfalsifiable and therefore supposedly unscientific. A more recent and thorough critique is Jon Elster's *Making Sense of Marx* (1985). Despite the title of his book, Elster finds more nonsense than sense in Marx. On the other side, however, is G.A. Cohen's penetrating and challenging response to such criticisms, *Karl Marx's Theory of History: A Defence* (1978).

Political Theory
and Politics

A former president of the United States often boasted that he had never taken a course in political science. It would be difficult to argue that he would have gained an advantage in competing for high office if he had formally studied the subject. Nonetheless, there can be little doubt of the relevance of political science to public affairs. As discussed in chapter 1, the primary value of social science lies not in providing the practical knowledge that ultimately must come from practice itself but in the exploration of systemic effects and other unintended consequences. This kind of knowledge is useful, indeed essential, to those who want to do more than simply prevail over their opponents and is why contemporary political leaders in most nations are surrounded by advisers trained in the social sciences.

Political science is relevant, and political theory is necessarily a part of political science. All efforts to explain political events and relate them to one another presuppose an understanding of why most people follow social conventions most of the time. This understanding rests on one's notion of what counts as rational human motivation, which in turn depends on one's view of human nature. Every student of politics, as well as every politician, must assume, however implicitly, this kind of knowledge. The intent of the preceding chapters has been to explicate alternative "conceptual paradigms" and explore their respective implications for how political and social scientists might define their subject matter and begin to make sense of political experience.

Social science is useful, perhaps even crucial, in accomplishing political ends. Yet the relevance of political theory to politics goes beyond its contribution to social science. The ends of politics are themselves subject to redefinition in political theory. Because one's conception of human nature provides expectations about rational priorities and the essential functions of political organization, it also defines both the limits and prospects of politics in achieving a social environment in which we can realize our human potential. This is the "normative" dimension of political theory.

The Tension between Political Theory and Politics

Political theorists typically accentuate the normative dimension in their interpretations of the classic works of political thought. Instead of emphasizing the utility of the classics in helping us to make sense of political phenomena, they tend to focus on the political ideals found within them. This emphasis on ideals serves to render the relevance of these works to the real world of politics somewhat problematic. Politics is a form of struggle and competition, and there is little reason to think that the possession of superior ideals necessarily imparts some sort of political advantage to one contestant over another. To the practical politician, discussion of the ideal ends of politics is likely to seem rather academic in the absence of any consideration of how such ends are to be realized. Yet questions of politics are usually ignored by political theorists.

This is true not only of contemporary scholars but also of the classic works of political thought they study. Indeed, with only one exception, the great political thinkers discussed in this book saw political struggle as unfortunate, if not a form of corruption. Each offered a nonconflictual conception of collective decision making. Aristotle, Locke, and Rousseau foresaw deliberation among like-minded citizens; Mill essentially agreed, expecting representative institutions to force contending parties to reach consensus through deliberation; Plato urged tutelage by the wise; Hobbes, Augustine, and Marx believed, each in his own way, that effective political power was inevitably autocratic. Only Machiavelli affirmed the inherent worth of political struggle, both for individuals capable of leadership and communities so fortunate as to have an open political system allowing such individuals to compete with one another without relying on coercion.

The reason political theorists typically have little positive to say about politics is that they usually are concerned with larger "constitutional" questions pertaining to the institutional and moral environment in which political struggle takes place. They tend to see their primary task in finding rational principles of political organization and defining the jurisdiction of legitimate political power. If a totally rational political system were possible, rational citizens would have no need to mobilize rival constituencies in order to establish appropriate political institutions. For insofar as constitutional principles are rational, there is a basis for a general consensus on their validity, and political struggle can be replaced by public deliberation.

There is, therefore, an elemental tension between politics and political theory. Although they may be concerned with the same things, they are very different activities. To the extent that political theory successfully discerns rational political priorities, political struggle should be superseded by consensus. Of course, many citizens may not comprehend the validity of rational principles, and political action may be necessary to implement or maintain a rational order, most likely through some combination of education and suppression. Politics may be necessary in such circumstances, but it is an unfortunate necessity. From this perspective, the sooner it is eliminated as a means of making collective decisions, the better. Collective decisions that can be made on the basis of deliberation and rational consensus should not be made by political influence any more than they should be made by brute force.

Political Theory and Constitutional Principles

This tension between political theory and politics is at least analogous, if not equivalent, to the friction between constitutional stipulations and political power. Whatever else they do, both political ideals and constitutional regulations serve to constrain the discretion of the politically ambitious. Indeed, constitutions inevitably reflect political ideals, and their effectiveness would seem to depend on consensus on either the proper ends of government or the criteria governments must meet before they are to be considered legitimate.

The analogy cannot be considered an identity, however, because some political ideals are simply incompatible with constitutionalism. Both St. Augustine and Marx, for instance, argue that all political power ultimately rests on coercion. For St. Augustine, any ideal supposedly legitimizing secular authority has to be arbitrary, and to think otherwise is not only wrong but sinful. For Marx, all specifically political ideals could only be forms of false consciousness, masking class domination.

And although Hobbes does not believe that political power ultimately rests on coercion, he denounces all attempts to hold political authority responsible to an ideal standard. From his perspective constitutionalism is a dangerous delusion, a certain source of political and social instability.

By far the greater number of political theorists in the West, however, have explicitly championed constitutional limits on political authority. Either governments are obliged to conform to some sort of higher law or they are required to foster essential human potential existing prior to any legal rights and obligations established by conventional authority. From this latter perspective, often identified as the "Modern" tradition of political thought, the only rational basis for governmental authority is the protection of human rights and the promotion of human freedom.

The "Classical" tradition of political thought, in contrast, is characterized by the affirmation of "natural law," derived from a natural order in which things are identified by their function in the larger whole. To define things by their purpose is called "teleological" definition, and in Classical political thought human beings have a natural end that they must fulfill in order to live satisfactory lives in accordance with the natural order of the universe. In Plato's variant of these assumptions we must live in accordance with reason if we are to live fulfilling lives, and the only way most could do so is through rule by "philosopher kings."

Aristotle, however, was skeptical that any human could completely comprehend the natural order of things, especially since the universe is still evolving toward some final cause. By his account, partial knowledge of the natural order is gained through reflection on experience. Consequently, the collective experience of tradition is likely to provide more certain knowledge than the unaided efforts of individuals, and there is little justification for rule by philosophers. The person most likely to live according to reason is the citizen who both understands the traditional constitution of the political community and is capable of embodying this knowledge in public service.

Despite their differences, Plato and Aristotle agreed that public policy was not a matter of will but of knowledge. Both were highly critical of democracy because they believed that democratic government is based on popular will, rather than objective principles of political right. More important in the present context, from their perspective constitutional government is possible only if based on objective principles that are true irrespective of anybody's will. If a constitution is no more than an advantageous agreement among individuals, it rests on nothing more than the collective might of those advantaged by it. And if a supposed constitution rests on might, rather than right, it cannot be expected to limit the political power on which it rests. It is then not really a constitution but a facade, probably intended to facilitate the exercise of power by giving it an aura of legitimacy.

Many contemporary proponents of the Classical tradition of political thought doubt that those who work within the Modern tradition can establish a defensible basis for constitutionalism. Having rejected the existence of a natural order that can serve as an objective guide in the conduct of human affairs, Modern political theorists are forced to turn to individual consent as the basis of political legitimacy. This is the reason some of the most prominent political thinkers in the Modern tradition resorted to the idea of a social contract in order to clarify their arguments. But if consent alone were all that mattered, it would be simply another way of referring to individual will, and the Classical critique of the Modern tradition obviously would be correct.

Actually the matter is not so simple. Consent means nothing unless it is given for rational reasons by rational people. The social contract theorists were concerned with the reasons, and under what circumstances, a rational person would be compelled to give consent, rather than with the concrete act of consenting. Hobbes claimed that a rational person would be willing to obey almost any government rather than face the risks associated with a collapse of authority. Locke and Rousseau, in contrast, could be a great deal more discriminating because they had, on the one hand, significantly loftier conceptions than Hobbes of the requisites for a human existence and, on the other, somewhat diminished views of the importance of political authority in securing these requisites. Consequently, both theorists could specify the proper jurisdiction of political authority and impose procedural rules on its exercise as necessary conditions for rational consent. Such stipulations are the essence of constitutional government, and it does not appear that the Modern tradition is inherently incompatible with constitutionalism.

There are, however, important differences in the constitutionalism associated with each of these two traditions of political thought. Rejecting the assumption of a natural order accessible at least in part to human reason, the Modern tradition necessarily rejects teleological conceptions of humanity. Instead, theorists working within the Modern tradition define humanity in terms of an essential capacity, rather than a predetermined end. For Rousseau, human beings were defined by their ability to be moral agents; for Locke, it was their ability to be rational producers. A legitimate political order is one in which this ability, however conceived, can be nurtured and amplified. Such an order is not discovered; it is invented. It is a project contrived by humans for humans, an imposition on an indifferent if not senseless universe. The ultimate end of politics becomes the expansion of human freedom through the creation of a more rational political and social order.

From the Classical perspective, political order is attained by conforming to the natural order of things. Politics should consist largely of adaptation, bringing the ever-changing particularities of the specific environment in line with the immutable truths of the natural order. From the Classical perspective, the Modern project asks too much of politics. The social and psychological complexities of human civilization cannot be remade according to plan. Any attempt to do so will inevitably generate startling unforeseen consequences and is likely to rationalize some very unpleasant ethical compromises.

Political Theory, Constitutional Principles, and Politics

This useful distinction between Classical and Modern political thought refers to the presence or absence of a metaphysical assumption. The Classical tradition is defined by the affirmation of a knowable natural order, of which we are a part, and the Modern tradition by its absence or irrelevance. Are the principles of political order invented, or are they found? Plato attempted to establish the existence of natural guidelines as an epistemological necessity, but rare is the scholar who thinks he succeeded. Contemporary proponents typically argue for acceptance of the assumption by alleging the awful consequences of its rejection. Much could be said about the implications of its acceptance or rejection, but in the present context the pertinent point is that it is an assumption, rather than a deduction, or even a conclusion.

Whether such an order exists does not seem subject to logical demonstration, any more than the particular conceptions of human nature underlying each of the conceptual paradigms discussed in previous chapters can be conclusively demonstrated to be valid or invalid. Political theorists deal with the axioms of political thought. The only test of an axiom is self-evidence, and familiarity is the most common reason something appears self-evident. One can attempt to discredit widely held assumptions by deducing bizarre implications from them, but the only tactic by which a theoretical axiom can be put forth as superior to a familiar alternative is to demonstrate that it allows one to do more. Demonstrations of this sort, however, are necessarily inconclusive because what one can accomplish depends at least as much on effort and skill as on one's conceptual tools. With conceptions of human nature, the inconclusiveness is even more acute because what one might want to accomplish is in part determined by who we think we are or ought to be.

Our inability to prove the superiority of one conceptual paradigm over all others does not mean that they are all equally valid or invalid. Nor does it follow that it makes no difference which of these ways of defining social and political reality is adopted. How scholars define their subject matter clearly has far-reaching implications for the questions they ask and the ways they attempt to answer them, just as the fundamental social outlook of political actors has far-reaching implications for what they want and how they think they might get it. The lack of a sure method of ascertaining the validity of the conceptual axioms of our social thought releases us neither from the necessity of affirming a conceptual paradigm nor from the responsibility of defending it.

In any case, the presumption that such a responsibility exists provides the rationale for this book. To defend our fundamental conceptual assumptions requires us to be able to articulate them, as well as understand the implications of thinking in terms of these rather than other categories. To do this we must understand alternative ways of looking at social and political reality, and I have attempted in previous chapters to present the most challenging alternatives in such a manner as to facilitate comparison with one another while accentuating both the distinctiveness and internal coherence of each. Some of the potential benefits for the student of understanding alternative political theories were mentioned in chapter 1. In these closing pages, I want to suggest that theoretical debate, despite its inconclusiveness, has some social benefit as well.

Unfortunately, I must begin with the acknowledgment that theoretical debate is to some extent subversive. For if theoretical debate is inherently inconclusive, a totally rational consensus on constitutional principles is not possible. Every functioning constitution must rest on some degree of consensus, but such a consensus cannot be the result of theoretical deliberation alone. Every constitutional consensus must be "political" as well as "theoretical."

It must be theoretical in the sense that a society must be able to articulate basic constitutional principles in order to promulgate and propagate them, as well as to defend them from skeptics. It must be political in the sense that the community must affirm its constitutional principles in the absence of any conclusive proof of their validity. By offering alternatives and exposing the logical tenuousness of received principles, theoretical debate is always to some degree inimical to constitutional consensus.

Political theorists generally do not exert much influence on public sentiments, and the threat their endeavor represents to constitutional stability is probably negligible in most circumstances. Political insignificance may be the most effectual claim for political tolerance, but my purpose is to suggest a more positive case based on the social benefits of theoretical criticism and debate. There are at least two arguments to support this case.

The first I take from John Stuart Mill, and pertains to the theoretical dimension of a constitutional consensus, the need for constitutional principles to be articulated and understood. By Mill's analysis, in the absence of serious debate even fundamental ideas will degenerate into conventional dogma, learned by rote, rather than really understood and taken seriously. Responding to criticism requires the elaboration of implications and the amplification of meaning. Widely held beliefs are more likely to maintain both their persuasiveness and their influence when intellectually defended than when imposed as orthodoxy by authority. Consequently, if one truly believes in the validity of constitutional principles, the inconclusiveness of theoretical debate presents more of an opportunity than a threat.

More fundamental, however, is the second argument for the social value of theoretical debate, which pertains to the political dimension of a constitutional consensus. There must be a political dimension because a constitutional consensus cannot be the result of rational deliberation alone. In the final analysis, the validity of basic constitutional principles simply has to be affirmed on faith, without benefit of conclusive verification. Yet this does not mean that such affirmation is irrational or that faith must be blind. Of course it often is blind and, when it is, it may more appropriately be referred to as "irrational" than "political." To be considered "political," the affirmation of constitutional principles must result from open competition among social alternatives.

In the first section of this chapter, I indicated that there is a tension between politics and political theory. When it is possible to establish rational consensus, there should be no need for political struggle. But the inconclusiveness of theoretical debate leads to a close, even symbiotic relationship between these types of endeavor. Indeed, their respective needs are so closely entwined that any attempt to eliminate theoretical debate will eventually require the repression of political opposition, of open political struggle.

Although theoretical and political tolerance probably have the same psychological roots, there is no need to resort to psychological assertions to establish the mutual dependence of politics and theoretical debate. The connection rests on the fact that theoretical debate can be terminated only by force. Given the impossibility of a conclusive rational theory of social and political affairs, it is also impossible to maintain a consensus by agreeing to avoid all argument over fundamentals. Conceivably, people agreeing on fundamentals could agree to leave technical matters of implementation to administrative technicians, at least insofar as they could agree on what qualifies as "technical." Yet it is impossible to do the reverse, to confine argument by mutual agreement to technical or relatively unimportant issues. For there simply is no way to avoid contention over whether proposals are purely technical or somehow compromise fundamental principles. Inevitably, even among those who share a general consensus on fundamentals, little issues periodically grow into big issues.

If constitutional issues are to be unsullied by politics, it must be by a suprapolitical imperative that supposedly justifies coercion of dissidents. Consequently, whenever theoretical discourse is monopolized by certified officials, we can expect opposition to be illegal, and open struggle, where it exists, to be military rather than political. Instead of political theorists, there will be priests, and instead of politicians, soldiers. I will not dwell on the social advantages of political struggle over military conflict; they are too obvious.

If opposition can be stifled and constitutional principles imposed on an acquiescent population, domination and stability are the rewards of military success. There are, however, costs. To the extent political order is secured by fear, any principles by which it might have been sustained are bound to be superfluous and futile. Corruption is inevitable. For the greatest enemies of constitutional principle are not alternative theoretical ideals, but cynicism and the unrestrained inclination to pursue short-term personal advantage. The inconclusiveness of theoretical debate must not obscure its political importance.

Selected Bibliography

Althusser, Louis. 1969. *For Marx*. London: Allen Lane.

Anglo, Sydney. 1969. *Machiavelli: A Dissection*. New York: Harcourt, Brace and World.

Arnhart, Larry. 1981. *Aristotle on Political Reasoning: A Commentary on the "Rhetoric."* DeKalb: Northern Illinois University Press.

Avineri, Shlomo. 1968. *The Social and Political Thought of Karl Marx*. London: Cambridge University Press.

Barker, Sir Ernest. 1959. *The Political Thought of Plato and Aristotle*. New York: Dover Publications.

Bathory, Peter Dennis. 1981. *Political Theory as Public Confession: The Social and Political Thought of St. Augustine of Hippo*. New Brunswick, N.J.: Transaction Books.

Berlin, Isaiah. 1948. *Karl Marx: His Life and Environment*. London: Oxford University Press.

Bluhm, William T. 1978. *Theories of the Political System: Classics of Political Thought and Modern Political Analysis*. Englewood Cliffs, N.J.: Prentice Hall.

Brecht, Arnold. 1959. *Political Theory: The Foundations of Twentieth-Century Political Thought*. Princeton: Princeton University Press.

Britton, Karl. 1969. *John Stuart Mill: Life and Philosophy*. New York: Dover Publications.

Brown, Peter. 1967. *Augustine of Hippo: A Biography*. Berkeley: University of California Press.

Burnyeat, M.F. 1985. "Sphinx without a Secret," *New York Review of Books* 32 (30 May).

Cassirer, Ernst. 1963. *The Question of Jean-Jacques Rousseau*. Bloomington: Indiana University Press.

Chapman, John W. 1956. *Rousseau—Totalitarian or Liberal?* New York: Columbia University Press.

Cobban, Alfred. 1934. *Rousseau and the Modern State*. London: Allen and Unwin.

Cohen, G.A. 1978. *Karl Marx's Theory of History: A Defence*. Princeton: Princeton University Press.

Condren, Conal. 1985. *The Status and Appraisal of Classic Texts: An Essay on Political Theory, Its Inheritance, and the History of Ideas*. Princeton: Princeton University Press.

Connolly, William E. 1993. *The Augustinian Imperative: A Reflection on the Politics of Morality*. Newbury Park, Calif.: Sage Publications.

Copleston, Frederick. 1955. *Thomas Aquinas*. London: Search Press.

Cowling, Maurice. 1963. *Mill and Liberalism*. Cambridge, England: Cambridge

University Press.

Cranston, Maurice. 1957. *John Locke: A Biography*. New York: Macmillan.

———. 1982. *Jean-Jacques: The Early Life and Work of Jean-Jacques Rousseau, 1712–1754*. New York: Norton.

———. 1991. *The Noble Savage: Jean-Jacques Rousseau, 1754–1762*. Chicago: University of Chicago Press.

Deane, Herbert A. 1963. *The Political and Social Ideas of St. Augustine*. New York: Columbia University Press.

de Grazia, Sebastian. 1989. *Machiavelli in Hell*. Princeton: Princeton University Press.

D'Entreves, Alexander Passerin. 1939. *The Medieval Contribution to Political Thought: Thomas Aquinas, Marsilius of Padua, Richard Hooker*. London: Oxford University Press.

Dunn, John. 1969. *The Political Thought of John Locke: An Historical Account of the Argument of the "Two Treatises of Government."* London: Cambridge University Press.

Easton, David. 1953. *The Political System: An Inquiry into the State of Political Science*. New York: Knopf.

Elshtain, Jean Bethke. 1981. *Public Man, Private Woman: Women in Social and Political Thought*. Princeton: Princeton University Press.

Elster, Jon. 1985. *Making Sense of Marx*. New York: Cambridge University Press.

Freedman, Robert. 1990. *The Marxist System: Economic, Political, and Social Perspectives*. Chatham, N.J.: Chatham House.

Germino, Dante. 1972. *Modern Western Political Thought: Machiavelli to Marx*. Chicago: Rand McNally.

Gilbert, Felix. 1965. *Machiavelli and Guicciardini: Politics and History in Sixteenth-Century Florence*. Princeton: Princeton University Press.

Gilby, Thomas. 1958. *The Political Thought of Thomas Aquinas*. Chicago: University of Chicago Press.

Gilson, Etienne. 1960. *The Christian Philosophy of Saint Augustine*. New York: Random House.

Gouldner, Alvin W. 1965. *Enter Plato: Classical Greece and the Origins of Social Theory*. New York: Basic Books.

Grabmann, Martin. 1963. *Thomas Aquinas: His Personality and Thought*. New York: Russell and Russell.

Grant, Ruth W. 1987. *John Locke's Liberalism*. Chicago: University of Chicago Press.

Grene, Marjorie. 1963. *A Portrait of Aristotle*. Chicago: University of Chicago Press.

Grimsley, Ronald. 1973. *The Philosophy of Rousseau*. New York: Oxford University Press.

Gunnell, John G. 1979. *Political Theory: Tradition and Interpretation*. Cambridge, Mass.: Winthrop.

Hale, J.R. 1960. *Machiavelli and Renaissance Italy*. New York: Macmillan.

Halevy, Elie. 1928. *The Growth of Philosophic Radicalism*. New York: Macmillan.

Hallowell, John. 1950. *Main Currents in Modern Political Thought*. New York: Holt, Rinehart and Winston.

Hamburger, Joseph. 1965. *Intellectuals in Politics: John Stuart Mill and the Philosophic Radicals.* New Haven: Yale University Press.

Himmelfarb, Gertrude. 1974. *On Liberty and Liberalism: The Case of John Stuart Mill.* New York: Knopf.

Hulliung, Mark. 1983. *Citizen Machiavelli.* Princeton: Princeton University Press.

Jaeger, Werner. 1948. *Aristotle: Fundamentals of the History of His Development.* Oxford, England: Oxford University Press.

Jaffe, Harry V. 1952. *Thomism and Aristotelianism: A Study of the Commentary by Thomas Aquinas on the Nicomachean Ethics.* Chicago: University of Chicago Press.

Johnston, David. 1986. *The Rhetoric of Leviathan: Thomas Hobbes and the Politics of Cultural Transformation.* Princeton: Princeton University Press.

Kendall, Willmore. 1941. *John Locke and the Doctrine of Majority-Rule.* Urbana: University of Illinois Press.

Klosko, George. 1986. *The Development of Plato's Political Theory.* New York: Methuen.

———. 1993. *History of Political Theory: An Introduction, Vol. I: Ancient and Medieval Political Theory.* New York: Holt, Rinehart and Winston.

———. 1995. *History of Political Theory: An Introduciton, Vol. II: Modern Political Theory.* New York: Holt, Rinehart and Winston.

Laslett, Peter. 1963. "Introduction." In John Locke, *Two Treatises of Government.* New York: Cambridge University Press.

Lichtheim, George. 1964. *Marxism: An Historical and Critical Study.* New York: Praeger.

Lord, Carnes. 1982. *Education and Culture in the Political Thought of Aristotle.* Ithaca: Cornell University Press.

McDonald, Lee Cameron. 1968. *Western Political Theory: From Its Origins to the Present.* New York: Harcourt, Brace and World.

MacIntyre, Alasdair. 1988. *Whose Justice? Which Rationality?* Notre Dame, Ind.: University of Notre Dame Press.

———. 1990. *Three Rival Versions of Moral Enquiry: Encyclopedia, Genealogy, Tradition.* Notre Dame, Ind.: University of Notre Dame Press.

Macpherson, C.B. 1964. *The Political Theory of Possessive Individualism: Hobbes to Locke.* Oxford, England: Oxford University Press.

Mansfield, Harvey C., Jr. 1989. *Taming the Prince: The Ambivalence of Modern Executive Power.* New York: Free Press.

Maritain, Jacques. 1951. *Man and the State.* Chicago: University of Chicago Press.

Masters, Roger D. 1989. *The Nature of Politics.* New Haven: Yale University Press.

Mazlish, Bruce. 1975. *James and John Stuart Mill: Father and Son in the Nineteenth Century.* New York: Basic Books.

Mehta, Uday Singh. 1992. *The Anxiety of Freedom: Imagination and Individuality in Locke's Political Thought.* Ithaca, N.Y.: Cornell University Press.

Melzer, Arthur M. 1990. *The Natural Goodness of Man: On the System of Rousseau's Thought.* Chicago: University of Chicago Press.

Meszaros, Istvan. 1970. *Marx's Theory of Alienation.* New York: Harper and Row.

Miller, James. 1984. *Rousseau: Dreamer of Democracy.* New Haven: Yale University Press.

Oakeshott, Michael. 1975. *Hobbes on Civil Association.* Oxford, England: Basil Blackwell.

Okin, Susan Moller. 1979. *Women in Western Political Thought.* Princeton: Princeton University Press.

Ollman, Bertell. 1971. *Alienation: Marx's Conception of Man in Capitalist Society.* Cambridge, England: Cambridge University Press.

Packe, Michael St. John. 1954. *The Life of John Stuart Mill.* New York: Macmillan.

Padover, Saul K. 1978. *Karl Marx: An Intimate Biography.* New York: McGraw-Hill.

Peters, Richard S. 1967. *Hobbes.* Harmondsworth, England: Penguin.

Pitkin, Hanna Fenichel. 1984. *Fortune Is a Woman: Gender and Politics in the Thought of Niccolò Machiavelli.* Berkeley: University of California Press.

Pocock, J.G.A. 1975. *The Machiavellian Moment: Florentine Political Thought and the Atlantic Republican Tradition.* Princeton: Princeton University Press.

Popper, Karl R. 1957. *The Open Society and Its Enemies.* London: Routledge and Kegan Paul.

Rees, John C. 1985. *John Stuart Mill's* On Liberty. New York: Oxford University Press.

Robson, John M. 1968. *The Improvement of Mankind: The Social and Political Thought of John Stuart Mill.* London: Routledge.

Rogow, Arnold A. 1986. *Thomas Hobbes: Radical in the Service of Reaction.* New York: Norton.

Ryan, Alan. 1970. *The Philosophy of John Stuart Mill.* London: Macmillan.

Sabine, George H. 1961. *A History of Political Theory.* New York: Holt, Rinehart and Winston.

Salkever, Stephen G. 1990. *Finding the Mean: Theory and Practice in Aristotelian Political Philosophy.* Princeton: Princeton University Press.

Shapin, Steven, and Simon Schaffer. 1985. *Leviathan and the Air Pump: Hobbes, Boyle, and the Experimental Life.* Princeton: Princeton University Press.

Shklar, Judith N. 1969. *Men and Citizens: A Study of Rousseau's Social Theory.* London: Cambridge University Press.

Sigmund, Paul E., ed. 1988. *St. Thomas Aquinas on Politics and Ethics.* New York: Norton.

Spragens, Thomas A., Jr. 1973. *The Politics of Motion: The World of Thomas Hobbes.* Lexington: University of Kentucky Press.

Strauss, Leo. 1952. *The Political Philosophy of Hobbes: Its Basis and Its Genesis.* Chicago: University of Chicago Press.

———. 1953. *Natural Right and History.* Chicago: University of Chicago Press.

———. 1958. *Thoughts on Machiavelli.* Glencoe, Ill.: Free Press.

———. 1964. *The City and Man.* Chicago: University of Chicago Press.

Strauss, Leo, and Joseph Cropsey, eds. 1987. *History of Political Philosophy.* Chicago: University of Chicago Press.

Swanson, Judith A. 1992. *The Public and the Private in Aristotle's Political Philosophy.* Ithaca: Cornell University Press.

Talmon, Jacob L. 1952. *The Rise of Totalitarian Democracy.* Boston: Beacon Press.

Taylor, A.E. 1922. *The Mind of Plato.* Ann Arbor: University of Michigan Press.

————. 1955. *Aristotle*. New York: Dover Publications.

Thompson, Dennis F. 1976. *John Stuart Mill and Representative Government*. Princeton: Princeton University Press.

Tucker, Robert. 1972. *Philosophy and Myth in Karl Marx*. Cambridge, England: Cambridge University Press.

Warrender, Howard. 1957. *The Political Philosophy of Hobbes: His Theory of Obligation*. Oxford, England: Oxford University Press.

Weisheipl, James A. 1974. *Friar Thomas d'Aquino: His Life, Thought, and Work*. Garden City, N.Y.: Doubleday and Company.

Wilson, Edmund. 1940. *To the Finland Station: A Study of the Writing and Acting of History*. New York: Harcourt, Brace.

Wolff, Robert Paul. 1968. *The Poverty of Liberalism*. Boston: Beacon Press.

Wolin, Sheldon S. 1960. *Politics and Vision: Continuity and Innovation in Western Political Thought*. Boston: Little, Brown.

Wood, Ellen Meiksins, and Neal Wood. 1978. *Class Ideology and Ancient Political Theory: Socrates, Plato, and Aristotle in Social Context*. Oxford, England: Blackwell.

Yack, Bernard. 1993. *The Problems of a Political Animal: Community, Justice, and Conflict in Aristotelian Political Thought*. Berkeley: University of California Press.

Index

Accountability, Machiavelli on, 94
Aggression, cause of, 108; and fear, 128
Aliens, needs of, 54
Anger, defined, 104
Apology (Plato), 15
Arguments, kinds of, 8
Aristocracies: advantages of, 42; defects of, 42; disadvantages of, 44; as unstable, 42, 44
Aristotle: and Aquinas, 66, 70; on natural law, 188; and politics of honor, 31–46; profile of, 31–32; on nature of reality, 66
Artisans, Marx on, 173–74
Art of War, The (Machiavelli), 84
Assumptions: basic theoretical, 3–4; classical, 190; modern, 190
Augustine, Saint: on human reason, 67, 71; on political power, 187; and politics of sin, 49–63; on primacy of faith, 66; profile of, 49–50
Authoritarian governments: defined, 163; as source of political instability, 163–64. *See also* Government(s)
Authority: function and organization of, Aquinas on, 72–77; function and organization of, Aristotle on, 38–40; function and organization of, Augustine on, 56–58; function and organization of, Hobbes on, 109–111; function and organization of, Locke on, 124–27; function and organization of, Machiavelli on, 90–93; function and organization of, Marx on, 176–77; function and organization of, Mill on, 160–63; function and organization of, Plato on, 21–25; function and organization of, Rousseau on, 141–44; knowledge as source of, 112; need for, Hobbes on, 108–9; patterns of, Rousseau on, 137; vs. power, 10. *See also* Collective authority; Governmental authority; Legislative authority; Political authority; Public authority

Beauty: permanence of, 19; politics of, 28
Bentham, Jeremy, 153, 155
Bible, Divine Law and, 71
Bliss, defined, 105
Bourgeoisie, 180; as economically irrelevant, 181
Boyle, Robert, 120

Calvin, John, 66
Capitalism: as deferred consumption, 180; internal contradiction in, 180–81; as primary means of production, 180; rise of, 179
Causes, 33
Character: and choices, 165; as defined by Mill, 156; as end of government, 142; and happiness, 159; and personal freedom, 167; politics of, 167
Choice: as based on faith, 52; and will, 52
Christendom: as focus for happy life, 69, 72; as highest human organization, 79
Christians, 50; dangers to rule by, 58; as pilgrims, 54; and salvation, 52–53
Church: function of, 55; as mission, 55–56; primary purpose of, 55; as universal institution, 75–76
Citizen(s): Aristotle defines, 39–40; civic commitment of, 136; responsibilities of, Hobbes on, 115; Rousseau on, 144
Citizenship: Aquinas on, 79–80; politics of, 149–50; requirements of, 39; rights of, in polity, 42–43
City of God, The (Augustine), 50